SRA
Language *through* Literature

Level 6

Terry Dodds

A Division of The McGraw-Hill Companies

Columbus, Ohio

W9-AAH-626

Contents

Introduction iii

Lesson 1   *The Golden Bracelet* by David Kherdian 1

Lesson 2   *The Dragon Kite* by Nancy Luenn 14

Lesson 3   *Androcles and the Lion* by Dennis Nolan 23

Lesson 4   *Pedro and the Monkey* by Robert D. San Souci 30

Lesson 5   *The Faithful Friend* by Robert D. San Souci 39

Lesson 6   *In the Beginning* by Virginia Hamilton 47

Lesson 7   *The Great Race* by David Bouchard 53

Lesson 8   *A Ring of Tricksters* by Virginia Hamilton 62

Lesson 9   *Medusa* by Deborah Nourse Lattimore 69

Lesson 10   *The Sea King's Daughter* by Aaron Shepard 77

Lesson 11   *Favorite Norse Myths* retold by Mary Pope Osborne 84

Lesson 12   *Kids at Work* by Russell Freedman 93

Lesson 13   *The Great Kapok Tree* by Lynne Cherry 107

Lesson 14   *The Most Beautiful Roof in the World* by Kathryn Lasky 116

Lesson 15   *The Missing 'Gator of Gumbo Limbo* by Jean Craighead George 122

Lesson 16   *The Jazz Man* by Mary Hays Weik 128

Lesson 17   *The Most Beautiful Place in the World* by Ann Cameron 138

Lesson 18   *Run Away Home* by Patricia C. McKissack 143

Lesson 19   *Number the Stars* by Lois Lowry 149

Lesson 20   *Red Scarf Girl* by Ji-Li Jiang 156

Appendix 164

Lists ISBNs and Publishers of Literature Selections

www.sra4kids.com

SRA/McGraw-Hill

A Division of The McGraw·Hill Companies

Copyright © 2002 by SRA/McGraw-Hill.

All rights reserved. Except as permitted under the United States
Copyright Act, no part of this publication may be reproduced or
distributed in any form or by any means, or stored in a database
or retrieval system, without the prior written permission of the
publisher, unless otherwise indicated.

Send all inquiries to:
SRA/McGraw-Hill
8787 Orion Place
Columbus, OH 43240-4027

Printed in the United States of America.

ISBN 0-07-572182-1

1 2 3 4 5 6 7 8 9 POH 06 05 04 03 02 01

What is Language through Literature?

The *Language through Literature* program is a series of direct instruction resource guides that will allow you to help your students make the important connection between basic language skills and literature. Most lessons are based on an easily available, excellent quality picture book or novel. Some are award-winning titles, and all have been chosen because they are of appropriate interest and reading level.

This Guide

This Level 6 guide is designed for you to use in classrooms with diverse student needs and various levels of reading abilities. Using the guide, you will introduce the students to basic literary structures such as a wide range of folk literature, problem-centered stories, descriptive stories, fiction and nonfiction, explaining stories, drama, and various forms of poetry. You will present grammar and the correct use of punctuation through short language skill development activities. As students are introduced to editing and proofreading strategies, they will bring written expression from draft to final copy. Through the easy-to-follow lesson scripting, you will encourage the students to ask questions as they learn about their world through literature. You will then present them with effective strategies for writing both fiction and nonfiction passages.

Application

As they complete the lessons, the students will develop a personal framework into which they can add new information and concepts. As this framework grows, the students will develop the ability to see complex patterns that are necessary for organizing information and concepts. This organizing of information into patterns makes it possible for students to react to and use new learning in a personal way. For example, as the students look for story patterns and study various literary genre in the books they read, they develop a sense of beginning, middle, and ending. Through the process of guided and critical literary analysis, your students will participate in discussions about more advanced literary concepts such as theme, personification, and figurative language.

Your students will be involved in activities and projects that are designed to allow them to interact successfully and enthusiastically with many different genres of children's literature including photographic journals, realistic fiction, folk literature, myths, fairy tales, poetry, songs, drama, biography, historical fiction, fantasy, adventure, mystery, history, and nonfiction. The students will have many opportunities to be speakers, listeners, and viewers. As you present the lessons, the students will be challenged to express their ideas individually, in small groups, or to the whole class. You can reinforce the conventions of being good listeners and speakers in every lesson. The lessons will help you introduce your students to a wide variety of media and technology that they can use for gaining information and presenting their ideas to others.

Scheduling

At Level 6 of *Language through Literature,* you will read a new book to the students during most picture book lessons. It is easy to fit the lessons into your classroom schedule. You may choose to teach a whole lesson in one day or break apart the activities and teach them over the course of a week. Following are some possible scheduling options.

Option 1

Teach a lesson over the course of a week. On Monday, teach the Language Skills Development portion of the lesson. On Tuesday, read the book aloud. On Wednesday, analyze the book. On Thursday, begin the activities. On Friday, complete the activities.

Option 2

Teach a lesson throughout the day. Use the short Language Skills Development portion of the lesson as an opening exercise for the school day, have a literature analysis time later in the morning, and complete a writing activity during an afternoon period.

Option 3

Designate one day each week as a literature day and teach an entire lesson. Note: If you choose this option, be aware that some lessons may need more than one day to complete. These lessons may be extended over more than one week.

Option 4

Teach strands from the program in one block. Here are some examples: (1) You might use the Language Skills Development strand as an opening exercise each day.
(2) Once the students become familiar with the basic editing and proofreading formats, you can expand upon and use them as a short daily exercise. (3) You can pull the folk literature, media, poetry, or mini-novel studies and teach them in a block as a mini-unit.

How Do I Present the Lessons?

The lessons in *Language through Literature* provide you with an organized pattern for analyzing literature with your class and for inviting students' responses to the literature. The engaging and well-illustrated picture books and novels in the program need little introduction, and the students will eagerly become involved with them. Through the lesson activities, they will learn critical thinking skills and how to analyze literature as well as material presented through media other than books. The lessons will also provide you with background information for literary forms, such as historical fiction, classical folk literature, legends, folktales, myths, poetry, biography, and fairy tales, to help in your presentation of the lessons.

Each lesson varies considerably in the amount of time it will take you to present it. You need to allow sufficient time for student responses, quality writing, and completion of other activities. The time required for the main part of each literature lesson is dependent upon the length of the book and the amount of time you allow for discussion. As your students continue to become more confident and competent writers, the time for written activities will vary greatly.

In some parts of the lesson, you will ask the students to respond chorally to a hand or voice signal. The choral responses will help the students maintain a higher level of active involvement in the lesson. At other times, you will call on a student or on different students to express their ideas.

Always have the book from the lesson available for the students to look at during free time. You might want to create a library corner where several copies of the book are available plus additional titles that are similar in topic or are by the same author or illustrator. Invite the students to make comparisons among the books. See each lesson for related titles.

Why Should I Use Picture Books with Older Students?

Many pictures books are highly sophisticated and intended for an older audience. Much of the art found in picture books may be considered works of art. Picture books may be used as a stimulus for discussion as well as a means for instilling art appreciation. Many picture books involve complex themes and stories from a wide array of cultures. They are a means of bringing the world into the imaginations of your students. Using picture books with older students is an easy means for showing character development, setting, and actions in a way that quickly advances a plot line.

How Do I Use the Mini-Novel Studies?

Mini-novel studies are specially designed for you to involve your students in interacting with longer chapter books in a variety of ways. A range of novels and activities have been provided from easy to difficult. Vocabulary development exercises and activities have been provided for you to use with your students. These mini-novel studies may be taught at anytime in the program or at a point in time that matches any curriculum topic you are studying.

A number of options may be used for having your students participate in mini-novel studies.

Option One:

Students participate in guided practice of the vocabulary, read the novel, and complete follow-up activities. If you select this option, each student will need a copy of the novel.

Option Two:

Teacher reads the novel aloud to the students and students complete the follow-up activities. If you select this option, you will need one copy of the novel.

Option Three:

Divide the class into small groups and have each group complete one of the mini-novel studies found in this program. Students may then rotate through the novel groups and have an opportunity to read all the novels over time. If you select this option, you will need as many copies of the novel as the size of your largest group.

Option Four:

Students read the novel independently as part of the class free choice reading program.

How Can I Use the Writing Process to Improve My Students' Writing?

Your students will have a number of opportunities to write original pieces of writing in this program. The language skill development strand of the program introduces your students to basic language skills that will enable them to bring their writing from draft to final copy.

The writing process in this program starts with you giving your students an opportunity to generate and share a wide variety of ideas before they write. The planning process is facilitated through the use of specially designed planning sheets and writing formats. Writing formats and planning sheets provide your students with organizers that will help them focus on a central idea and to write stories that include important story elements such as characters, setting, problem, attempts at solution, and solution. Planning sheets may also be used by your students as an evaluation tool to determine if they have achieved the purpose for writing.

As your students revise, edit, and proofread their writing, you should encourage them to evaluate their own and the writing of others. Have your students work with editing and proofreading partners, so that they learn to help others apply the conventions of standard English and that they learn to comment constructively on the work of others.

Expect your students to spell words taught in formal spelling lessons or that are found on class charts correctly and to apply the grammar, usage, and punctuation strategies taught in the program to their own writing. Encourage your students to use references such as dictionaries, thesauruses, charts, and word lists to find information and the correct spelling of words.

How Do I Motivate My Students to Read?

It is recommended that your students participate in a Free Choice Reading Program throughout their participation in this program. Additional titles have been provided for each literature selection as well as a bibliography of interesting books (Lesson 1) that are at a range of reading levels.

Language Skill Development

Correct Use of Semicolons

Time Required: 15 minutes

When two complete sentences are about the same idea, you can sometimes join them using a punctuation mark called a **semicolon.** When two complete sentences are about the same idea, how can you join them? (Signal.) *With a semicolon.* (Draw a semicolon on the chalkboard.) This mark is called a semicolon.

(Write on the chalkboard: **Tasha's dog hates going to the vet. He howls whenever Tasha brings him in for a checkup.**) Read the first sentence aloud. (Signal.) *Tasha's dog hates going to the vet.* Is this a complete sentence? (Signal.) *Yes.* Read the second sentence aloud. (Signal.) *He howls whenever Tasha brings him in for a checkup.* Is this a complete sentence? (Signal.) *Yes.*

Both sentences tell about the idea of Tasha's dog hating to go to the vet, so you can join the two sentences together with a semicolon. (Erase the period after **vet** and insert a semicolon.) When you join two sentences with a **semicolon,** the sentence after the semicolon does not begin with a capital letter. (Put in the proofreading mark—a line through the letter—that shows the **H** should not be capitalized.) Now read the combined sentence aloud. (Signal.) *Tasha's dog hates going to the vet; he howls whenever Tasha brings him in for a checkup.*

(Write on the chalkboard: **The row of birch trees fell down in the storm. Many other trees were also damaged.**) Read the first sentence aloud. (Signal.) *The row of birch trees fell down in the storm.* Is this a complete sentence? (Signal.) *Yes.* Read the second sentence aloud. (Signal.) *Many other trees were also damaged.* Is this a complete sentence? (Signal.) *Yes.*

Both sentences tell about the idea of a storm blowing down trees, so you can join the two sentences with a semicolon. (Erase the period after **storm** and insert a semicolon.) When you join two sentences with a semicolon, the sentence after the semicolon does not begin with a capital letter. (Put in the proofreading mark that shows the **M** should not be capitalized.) Now read the combined sentences aloud. (Signal.) *The row of birch trees fell down in the storm; many other trees were also damaged.*

Activity

Correct Use of Semi-colons

Time Required: 10 minutes
Materials Required: BLM 1A, one copy for each student

Procedure

1. When you see two complete sentences, decide if they tell about the same idea and can be joined with a semicolon. Rewrite the sentences correctly using a semicolon whenever possible.
2. On the last line, try to think of two sentences of your own that can be joined with a semicolon.
3. (Circulate, ensuring that students are completing task correctly.)

Literature

Preparation: Compile a classroom library of trade books with folk literature from various cultures. Include folktales, fairy tales, myths, tall tales, fables, legends, creation stories, trickster tales, and pourquoi tales. Selections have been recommended throughout lessons 1 to 10 as well as in the bibliography found at the end of this lesson.

Materials required: A map of the world

> **Note:** After a class discussion of the selected book, an independent reading option of a second book is recommended. The books listed follow similar plot, characterization, and themes. You may wish to have your students read the recommended books independently (or in pairs or groups) and compare and contrast the optional selection by modeling their chart summaries (BLM 1B) on the chart completed during class discussion.
>
> **Note:** Prepare a cumulative class chart following the sample given below. This chart is to be filled in during each literature lesson. Students will have personal versions of this chart (see BLM 1B) that they may fill in from the completed class version and add to with their own summaries during the independent reading section outlined above.

Folk Literature Summary Chart

Title	Place of Origin	Genre	Purpose of Tale	Cultural values, morals, and character traits portrayed	Theme

For the next several weeks we are going to read and discuss folk literature from many cultures. Folk literature means stories that have been told for many years and handed down through many generations of people. Hundreds of years ago, storytellers were very important because there were no books. The stories for each culture were told aloud and memorized.

Many folktales are told for a purpose. Some tales tell about the creation of the world, others explain, some entertain, and some teach us a lesson.

The tales that we will be reading have four main purposes. Your job will be to decide which one of the four purposes fits the story that you are hearing or reading.

The purpose of some stories is to tell about the creation of the world. These stories are called **creation myths.** What is the purpose of a creation myth? (Signal.) *To tell about the creation of the world.*

The second purpose of some stories is to explain how things came to be. **Explaining stories** tell how natural phenomena, like lakes, stars, and mountains, came to be. These stories were told before science was able to explain why our world is the way it is today. What are stories that tell about how things came to be called? (Signal.) *Explaining stories.*

Trickster tales are another kind of story you will read. The purpose of trickster tales is to entertain. They tell about animals that use sneaky, tricky ways to get what they want. What is the purpose of a trickster tale? (Signal.) *To entertain.*

Sometimes the purpose of a story is to teach a lesson. Stories that teach a lesson often give advice on how to live a good, happy, and safe life. What are stories that give us advice called? (Signal.) *Stories that teach a lesson.*

Let's review the four purposes for folk literature. The first purpose for folk literature is: (Signal. Hold up one finger for each purpose.) *To tell about the creation of the world.* The second purpose is: (Signal.) *To explain how things came to be.* The third purpose is: (Signal.) *To entertain.* And the fourth purpose is: (Signal.) *To teach a lesson.* (Repeat until firm.)

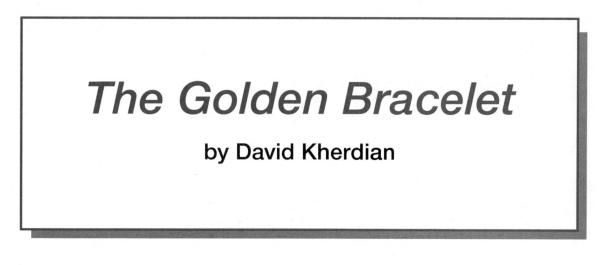

The Golden Bracelet
by David Kherdian

Examining the Book

This is the first book that we are going to read and discuss. (Point to the title.) Read the title of the book. (Signal.) *The Golden Bracelet.* (Record on class chart. Point to the author's name on the cover.) Who is the author of this book? (Call on a student. *David Kherdian.)* (Point to the illustrator's name on the cover.) Who is the illustrator of *The Golden Bracelet?* (Call on a student. *Nonny Hogrogian.)*

Today's story is from Armenia. (Show students the location of Armenia on a world map.) Where is this story from? (Signal.) *Armenia.* (Record on class chart.) There are many different versions of this Armenian story, but David Kherdian wrote the version of the story that we will read today.

The word **genre** tells what kind of story it is. What does the word genre tell? (Signal.) *What kind of story it is. The Golden Bracelet* is a folktale. What kind of story is *The Golden Bracelet?* (Signal.) *A folktale.* So, what genre is *The Golden Bracelet?* (Signal.) *A folktale.* (Record on chart.)

A folktale is a story that has been told by people for a long time. What is a folktale? (Signal.) *A story that has been told by people for a long time.*

Making Predictions

The Golden Bracelet is a folktale that takes place in Armenia. It involves learning a craft and one of the main characters getting out of trouble. Raise your hand if you can make a prediction about what will happen in this story. Tell about the craft, what trouble you think the character will get into, and how he gets out of trouble. (Call on different students. Accept two or three responses.)

What do you think the golden bracelet is? (Call on different students. Accept two or three responses.)

Predict the purpose of this folktale, based on what you already know about the story. Do you think it will be a creation myth, an explaining story, a trickster tale to entertain, or a story that teaches a lesson? Give a reason to support your prediction. (Call on different students. Accept reasonable responses.)

Reading the Book

I'm going to read this book aloud to you and show you the illustrations. (Read the book with minimal interruptions—this ensures that the students hear the story in its entirety, thus helping them develop a better sense of story.)

OR

You may also wish to have your students take turns reading parts of the story aloud to classmates.

(Remind students of the conventions of being effective speakers:

    Use appropriate rate, volume, and tone.

    Speak clearly and project your voice.

    Make eye contact with your audience.

    Use gestures and expression to make your speaking more interesting.)

(Effective listeners:

    Listen attentively.

    Face and make eye contact with the speaker.

    Remember what the speaker says.

    Raise their hands if they have a question or wish to make a comment.)

Occasionally you may find it beneficial to discuss parts of the story that are complicated or that have unfamiliar vocabulary. Encourage students to check the illustrations, the structures of words, and context to help them decipher unknown words and their meanings.)

Literary Analysis

The **plot** of a story tells what happened. What does the plot of a story tell? (Signal.) *What happened.* The plot of a story gives it a beginning, middle, and end. What does the plot of a story give it? (Signal.) *A beginning, middle, and end.*

The beginning tells about the setting of the story. The setting of a story tells where and when the story happens. What does the setting tell? (Signal.) *Where and when the story happens.* Where does this story happen? (Signal.) *Armenia.* When does this story happen? (Call on a student. Idea: *In an ancient time.*)

The most important characters in a story are called the **main characters.** What do we call the most important characters in a story? (Signal.) *The main characters.* What does the beginning of a story tell about? (Signal.) *The main characters that are in the story.* Who are the main characters in *The Golden Bracelet*? (Call on different students. Ideas: *Prince Haig; Anahid; Zilnago.*) What kind of person was Prince Haig? (Call on different students. Ideas: *Lazy; indolent; fun-loving; adventuresome; smart; skillful at weaving.*) What kind of person was Zilnago? (Call on different students. Ideas: *Evil; sly; greedy.*) What kind of person was Anahid? (Call on different students. Ideas: *Graceful; good-hearted; intelligent; skillful at weaving; wise.*)

Story Problem

The beginning of a story often has a problem that changes the everyday life of at least one of the characters. What was Prince Haig's problem at the beginning of the story? (Call on a student. Idea: *He fell in love with Anahid, but she refused to marry him.*) The **cause** of an event is a person or thing that makes something happen. What's the cause of an event? (Signal.) *A person or thing that makes something happen.* What was the cause of Prince Haig's problem at the beginning of the story? (Call on a student. Idea: *Anahid wouldn't marry Prince Haig unless he learned a useful trade.*) What is a Golden Bracelet? (Call on a student. Idea: *A special skill that a person learns and never forgets.*)

The **cause** of an event produces an **effect.** What does the cause of an event produce? (Signal.) *An effect.* An **effect** is the result of the cause. What's an effect? (Signal.) *The result of the cause.* What was the effect of Anahid's refusal to marry Prince Haig unless he mastered a craft? (Call on a student. Idea: *He decided on a craft and became a master weaver of gold cloth.*) Why did the king and queen predict that Prince Haig would not succeed at mastering a craft? (Call on a student. Ideas: *Prince Haig was lazy and fun-loving; they didn't think he would have the discipline to learn a skill.*)

What major problem did Prince Haig and Anahid encounter after they ascended the throne? (Call on a student. Idea: *Vartan, Prince Haig's friend, disappeared and never returned.*) What did Prince Haig do to find Vartan? (Call on different students. Ideas: *The king and queen sent out many search parties; Prince Haig disguised himself as a peasant artisan and traveled the kingdom looking for Vartan while Anahid ruled the kingdom alone.*) What had happened to Vartan? (Call on a student. Idea: *He had been imprisoned by the sorcerer Zilnago and forced to work as a slave.*) How did Prince Haig use his head and his skills to rescue himself and his friend? (Call on a student. Idea: *He agreed to weave gold cloth for the greedy sorcerer, and he wove a secret message and a map into the fabric to send to Anahid.*)

The end of the story tells what finally happens. This is called the **resolution** of the story. What do we call what finally happens in a story? (Signal.) *The resolution.* The resolution is often the solution to the problem. How did Anahid react when Zilnago showed her the golden cloth? (Call on different students. Ideas: *She tried to stay calm; she was afraid; she knew Zilnago was an evil man.*) What clue did Anahid notice that showed her there was a secret message in the cloth? (Call on a student. Idea: *Prince Haig had woven a golden bracelet into the upper right corner of the cloth.*)

Theme

The **theme** of a story tells the author's purpose for writing the story. Themes often convey truth and values and provide meaning to the plot of a story.

What do you think is the theme of *The Golden Bracelet*? (Call on different students. Idea: *Learning a useful skill can be a helpful asset in life. It may save your life.*)

Metaphor

When one idea is described as being something else to make a comparison, it is called a **metaphor.** What is it called when one idea is described as being something else to make a comparison? (Signal.) *A metaphor.*

(Write on the chalkboard: **Her hands were ice.**) Read the sentence aloud. (Signal.) *Her hands were ice.* Think carefully. Were her hands really ice? (Signal.) *No.* This metaphor means that her hands are so cold that they can be compared to ice, but they aren't really ice.

(Write on the chalkboard: **His voice was honey.**) Read the sentence aloud. (Signal.) *His voice was honey.* Think carefully. Was his voice really honey? (Signal.) *No.* The metaphor means that his voice sounds so smooth and sweet that it can be compared to honey, but it isn't really honey. Raise your hand if you can think of another metaphor. (Call on different students. Accept appropriate responses.)

(Turn to the page where Anahid explains what a Golden Bracelet means in her village. Read the second paragraph aloud.) Is the Golden Bracelet that the villagers treasure an actual metal loop that can be worn around a person's wrist? (Signal.) *No.* Raise your hand if you can explain in your own words what a Golden Bracelet really is. (Call on a student. Accept reasonable response.)

In this folktale, a Golden Bracelet is a metaphor for a skill or trade that a person learns and is good at. What is a Golden Bracelet a metaphor for? (Signal.) *A skill or trade that a person learns and is good at.* A person who knows an important skill is a valuable asset to his or her community.

Summarizing the Literary Analysis

Let's remember some of the things we learned about *The Golden Bracelet*, and I'll write them down for you.

What is the purpose of this folktale? (Call on a student. Idea: *To teach a lesson.* Record on chart.)

What are some of the cultural values of Anahid's village? (Call on a student. Idea: *Everyone should learn a craft, which they call a Golden Bracelet, to help him or her through life.* Record on chart.)

Is there a moral in this story? (Call on a student. Idea: *Stay calm and use your head to help you escape trouble.* Record on chart.)

Who are the main characters in this story? (Call on different students. Ideas: *Prince Haig, Anahid, Zilnago.*) What are some character traits of each of these characters? (Call on different students. Ideas: *Prince Haig is fun-loving, adventurous, smart; Anahid is intelligent, good-hearted, wise; Zilnago is sneaky, evil, cruel.*)

What is the theme of the story? (Call on a student. Idea: *Learning a useful skill can be a helpful asset in life. It may save your life.* Record on chart.)

BLM 1A   Read the sentences in each item. Decide if they tell about the same idea and can be joined with a semicolon. Rewrite the sentences that may be joined with a semicolon using correct punctuation. On the last line, write two sentences of your own that use a semicolon.

1.   Ms. Anderson works as a secret agent. Her code name is Red Robin.

_____

2.   Elizabeth enjoyed swimming. She baby-sat at night.

_____

3.   Kung Fu is a martial art that requires self-control. Discipline and agility are two other skills that are needed.

_____

_____

4.   Blue jeans are popular all over the world. They are a favorite fashion internationally.

_____

_____

5.   Louis spent many hours at the gym. He was trying to build big biceps.

_____

6.   Kirk never took exercise seriously. He worked at two jobs to support his family.

_____

_____

7.   Cheese and broccoli are packed with calcium. This mineral keeps teeth and bones strong and healthy.

_____

_____

8.   _____

_____

9.   _____

_____

© SRA/McGraw-Hill. Permission is granted to reproduce this page for classroom use.

FOLK LITERATURE SUMMARY CHART

Title	Place of Origin	Genre	Purpose of Tale	Cultural values, morals, and character traits portrayed	Theme

© SRA/McGraw-Hill. Permission is granted to reproduce this page for classroom use.

Free Choice Reading Program (Lessons 1–20)

Materials Required: Selection of books from various levels and genre for students to read independently. Choose books from literature selections, additional titles list and from the bibliography found on page 12 or any other titles that are suitable to the reading and interest level of the students.

(Introduce students to the Free Choice Reading Program. This may be a designated silent reading period of 15 to 30 minutes or assigned as homework from reading resources other than the classroom reader. Brief individual conferences may be held with students during this silent reading time by the teacher, teaching assistants, or volunteers. Generic questions may be asked that do not require the person conducting the conference to have read the entire book.)

(Show students a selection of books. It is important to give "book talks" throughout the program to keep students interested in reading a variety of authors and genres.) As you become more independent readers, it is important to read a greater variety of books. These are books that I think you can read independently. (Challenge students to read as many different genres and authors as possible. As students read in the various genres, add the distinguishing characteristics of each genre to the cluster. Encourage students to discuss the styles of different authors.)

(Introduce students to the concept of a reading log. Give them the following format for keeping a record of their free choice reading:)

Date started: _____ Date completed: _____

Title: _____ Author: _____

Genre: _____

Distinguishing features of genre: _____

What parts of this story make it a (write name of genre): _____

How difficult was this book?

(Please circle your choice.)   Easy   Just Right   Too Difficult

Explain what you like about this author's style. _____

If you were a literary critic, would you recommend this book? Tell why or why not.

If you were allowed to change this book, what would you change? Explain why.

Recommendations for Free Choice Reading Program (Grade Six)

Grade Five to Six

Avi *The True Confessions of Charlotte Doyle* (Historical Fiction) RL 5.3 Newbery Medal Winner

Cleary, Beverly *The Mouse and the Motorcycle* (Fiction) RL 5.1

Cleaver, Vera and Bill *Where the Lilies Bloom* (Fiction) RL 5.2

Coatsworth, Elizabeth Jane *The Cat Who Went to Heaven* (Fable) RL 5.9 Newbery Medal Winner

Cox, Clinton *Come All You Brave Soldiers: Blacks in the Revolutionary War* (History) RL 5.0

Curtis, Christopher Paul *The Watsons Go to Birmingham—1963* (Historical Fiction) RL 5.0

Doyle, Sir Arthur Conan *Adventures of Sherlock Holmes* (Illustrated version) (Mystery) RL 5.7

Fleischman, Sid *By the Great Horn Spoon!* (Historical Fiction) RL 5.1

George, Jean Craighead *Julie's Wolf Pack* (Fiction) RL 5.7

Gutman, Dan *The Kid Who Ran for President* (Realistic Fiction)

Hesse, Karen *Out of the Dust* (Poetry) RL 5.3

Jacques, Brian *Redwall* (Fiction-Hero Quest) RL 5.6

Konigsberg, E.L. *The View From Saturday* (Realistic Fiction) RL 5.9 Newbery Medal Winner

Krull, Kathleen *Wilma Unlimited* (Biography) RL 5.1

Lauber, Patricia *Painters of the Caves* (Non-fiction) RL 5.8

Levine, Ellen *If you Traveled West in a Covered Wagon* (Historical fiction) RL 5.2

Murphy, Jim *A Young Patriot: The American Revolution as Experienced by One Boy* (Fiction)

O'Dell, Scott *The Black Pearl* (Legend) RL 5.4 Newbery Medal Honor Winner

Paterson, Katherine *The Sign of the Chrysanthemum* (Historical Fiction) RL 5.0

Spinelli, Jerry *Wringer* (Contemporary Fiction) RL 4.5 Newberry Medal Honor Winner

Grade Six to Seven

Bowen, Gary *Stranded at Plimouth Plantation, 1626* (Historical fiction-diary) RL 6.4

Brink, Carol Ryrie *Caddie Woodlawn* (Historical Fiction) RL 6.0

Burnett, Frances Hodgson *The Secret Garden* (Fiction) RL 6.3

Cameron, Eleanor *The Wonderful Flight to the Mushroom Planet* (Science Fiction) RL 6.3

de Angeli, Marguerite *The Door in the Wall* (Fiction-hero quest) RL 6.2 Newberry Award Winner

Hart, Avery & Mantell, Paul *Pyramids!* (Non-fiction)

McCaffrey, Anne *Dragonsong* (Science Fiction) RL 6.8

Paulsen, Gary *The Voyage of the Frog* (Fiction-survival story) RL 6.0

Snyder, Zilpha Keatley *The Egypt Game* (Mystery) RL 6.4 Newberry Medal Honor Winner

Sperry, Armstrong *Call it Courage* (Fiction-adventure) RL 6.2 Newberry Medal Honor Winner

Swarthout, Glendon and Kathryn *Whichaway* (Fiction-survival story) RL 6.0

Warren, Andrea *Orphan Train Rider: One Boy's True Story* (Biography) RL 6.1

For Advanced Readers (Grades 7+)

Baker, Rachel *The First Woman Doctor* (Biography) RL 7.9

Carter, Forrest *Education of Little Tree* (Autobiography)

Eckert, Allan W. *Incident at Hawk's Hill* (Historical fiction) RL 7.2 Newberry Medal Honor Winner

Freedman, Russell *The Wright Brothers* (Non-fiction) RL 7.7 Newberry Medal Honor Winner

North, Sterling *Rascal* (Realistic Animal Story) RL 7.1

Hughes, Monica *What If...?* (Science Fiction) RL 7.0

Lawson, Robert *Mr. Revere and I* (Historical Fiction) RL 7.5

Sakurai, Gail *The Louisana Purchase* (Historical Fiction) RL 7.4

Bibliography of Folk Literature

Ada, Alma Flor *The Three Golden Oranges*

Choi, Yangsook *The Sun Girl and the Moon Boy*

Delacre, Lulu *Golden Tales: Myths, Legends and Folktales from Latin America*

Fisher, Leonard Everett *Gods and Goddesses of the Ancient Maya*

Hamilton, Virgina *The People Could Fly*

Kipling, Rudyard *Just So Stories*

Knappert, Jan *Kings, Gods & Spirits from African Mythology*

Kurtz, Jane *Miro in the Kingdom of the Sun*

Lewis, Paul Owen *Frog Girl*

McBratney, Sam *Celtic Myths*

McCaughrean, Geraldine *Myths and Legends of the World*

McDermott, Gerald *Anansi the Spider*

McDermott, Gerald *Arrow to the Sun*

Morley, Jacqueline *Greek Myths*

Moore Christopher and Balit, Christina *Ishtar and Tammuz*

Ober, Hal *How Music Came to the World*

Orlando, Louise *African Folktales*

San Souci, Robert D. *The Samurai's Daughter*

San Souci, Robert D. *The Secret of the Stones*

Shulevitz, Uri *The Treasure*

Thompson, Vivian L. *Hawaiian Myths of Earth, Sea, and Sky*

Toye, William and Elizabeth Cleaver *The Mountain Goats of Temlaham*

Walker, Paul Robert *Bigfoot and Other Legendary Creatures*

Wood, Audrey *The Rainbow Bridge*

Yolen, Jane *Sky Dogs*

Lesson 2

Language Skill Development
Using Commas with Conjunctions
Time Required: 15 minutes

A **conjunction** is a small word that joins two complete sentences. What is a word that joins two complete sentences called? (Signal.) *A conjunction.* (Write on the chalkboard: **and, but, or, nor, so**. Point to the list of words.) Some conjunctions that are common are written here. Read the list aloud. (Signal.) *And, but, or, nor, so.*

(Write on the chalkboard: **Lisa was a fast writer. She was a good speller too.**) Read the first sentence aloud. (Signal.) *Lisa was a fast writer.* Is this a complete sentence? (Signal.) *Yes.* Read the second sentence aloud. (Signal.) *She was a good speller too.* Is this a complete sentence? (Signal.) *Yes.*

Let's join these two sentences with the conjunction **and.** (Write on the chalkboard: **Lisa was a fast writer and she was a good speller too.**) When you use a conjunction to join two complete sentences, the conjunction must be introduced by a comma. With what must you introduce the conjunction? (Signal.) *A comma.* (Insert a comma after **writer.**) Now read the sentence aloud. (Signal.) *Lisa was a fast writer, and she was a good speller too.*

(Write on the chalkboard: **Dale wanted to go to the mall. The mall was closed.**) Read the first sentence aloud. (Signal.) *Dale wanted to go to the mall.* Is this a complete sentence? (Signal.) *Yes.* Read the second sentence aloud. (Signal.) *The mall was closed.* Is this a complete sentence? (Signal.) *Yes.*

Let's join these two sentences with the conjunction **but.** (Write on the chalkboard: **Dale wanted to go to the mall but the mall was closed.**) When you use a conjunction to join two complete sentences, the conjunction must be introduced by a comma. With what must you introduce the conjunction? (Signal.) *A comma.* (Insert a comma after **mall.**) Now read the sentence aloud. (Signal.) *Dale wanted to go to the mall, but the mall was closed.*

Activity

> ### Title: Practice using Conjunctions
> Time Required: 10 minutes
> Materials Required: BLM 2, one copy for each student

Procedure

1. Combine each pair of sentences using a conjunction. Use the words **and, but, or, nor, so.**

2. Rewrite the sentence on the lines below. What will you use to introduce the conjunction? (Signal.) *A comma.*

3. On the last line, write a sentence of your own using a conjunction. Write it on the lines provided.

4. (Circulate, ensuring that students are completing the task correctly.)

Literature

The Dragon Kite
by Nancy Luenn

Materials required: A map of the world
Folk Literature Summary Chart started in Lesson 1

> **Note:** After a class discussion of the selected book, an independent reading option of a second book is recommended. The books listed follow similar plot, characterization, and themes. You may wish to have your students read the recommended book independently (or in pairs or groups) and compare and contrast the optional selection by modeling their chart summaries (BLM 1B) on the chart completed during class discussion.

Many folktales are told for a purpose. Let's review the four purposes for folk literature. The first purpose for folk literature is: (Signal. Hold up one finger for each purpose.) *To tell about the creation of the world.* The second purpose is: (Signal.) *To explain how things came to be.* The third purpose is: (Signal.) *To entertain.* And the fourth purpose is: (Signal.) *To teach a lesson.* (Repeat until firm.)

Examining the Book

This is the next book that we are going to read and discuss. (Point to the title.) Read the title of the book. (Signal.) *The Dragon Kite.* (Record on class chart. Point to the author's name on the cover.) Who is the author of this book? (Call on a student. *Nancy Luenn.* Point to the illustrator's name on the cover.) Who is the illustrator of *The Dragon Kite*? (Call on a student. *Michael Hague.*)

Today's story is from Japan. (Show students the location of Japan on a world map.) Japan is an island country. Mt. Fuji is a very tall and famous mountain in Japan. What is the origin of this story? (Signal.) *Japan.* (Record on class chart.) The main character in this story is a historical figure who lived in the late 1600s or early 1700s. His real name was Ishikawa, and he was a thief. There are several different versions of this Japanese story that tell about Ishikawa's daring thefts, but Nancy Luenn wrote the version of the story that we will read today.

The genre of *The Dragon Kite* is a folktale. What genre is *The Dragon Kite*? (Signal.) *A folktale.* (Record on chart.)

The genre of *The Dragon Kite* is a legend as well, because the story is based on a historical figure who existed a long time ago. What other genre is *The Dragon Kite*? (Signal.) *A legend.* (Record on chart.) A legend often exaggerates real events or people. What is a legend? (Signal.) *A story that exaggerates real events or people.*

Making Predictions

The Dragon Kite is a folktale and legend that takes place in Japan and involves a historical figure who is a thief and a daring robbery. Raise your hand if you can make a prediction about what will happen in this story. Tell about the theft, what trouble you think the character will get into, and how he gets out of trouble. (Call on different students. Accept two or three responses.)

(Open up the front and back covers of the book so that students see the picture in its entirety.) Raise your hand if you would like to predict what is happening in the part of the story that the cover is illustrating. Tell us what part of the illustration gives you an idea about what is happening. (Call on different students. Accept two or three responses.)

What do you think the dragon kite is? (Call on different students. Accept two or three responses.)

Predict the purpose of this folktale and legend, based on what you already know about the story. Do you think it will be a creation myth, an explaining story, a trickster tale to entertain, or a story that teaches a lesson? Give a reason to support your prediction. (Call on different students. Accept reasonable responses.)

Reading the Book

Choose one of the two options presented in Lesson 1 for reading the book. If students read parts of the story aloud, remind them of the conventions for being an effective speaker and listener found in Lesson 1.

Occasionally, you may find it beneficial to discuss parts of the story that are complicated or that have unfamiliar vocabulary. Encourage students to check the illustrations, the structures of words, and context to help them decipher unknown words and their meanings.)

Literary Analysis

(Read aloud the author's note inside the front cover of the book.) After Ishikawa's theft of the dolphin fins, what did the Shogun do to prevent any further robberies at Nagoya Castle? (Call on different students. Ideas: *He forbade anyone to build large kites; iron cages were built around the golden dolphins.*) Did these safety measures work? (Signal.) *No.*

Let's talk about the setting of this folktale. Where does this story happen? (Signal.) *In Japan.* When does this legend happen? (Call on a student. Idea: *When the Shogun was master of all Japan.*)

Is there anything in the illustrations or the story itself that tells you about the landscape, clothing, or culture in Japan in the ancient time that this folktale and legend takes place? (Call on different students. Ideas: *Bamboo trees; cherry blossom trees; the ocean; a snow-topped mountain; colorful kimonos; clothing; kites; unique names of the characters.*) Think about the next three questions that I am going to ask. Do you think that these things might still be important to the culture of Japan today? What do you think might have changed? What might have stayed the same? (Call on different students. Ideas: *There are probably still bamboo and cherry blossom trees; the mountain and ocean are still there, but people probably wear modern clothes.*)

Who are the main characters in *The Dragon Kite?* (Call on different students. Idea: *Ishikawa; Katsuta the kite-maker.*) What kind of person was Ishikawa at the beginning of the story? (Call on different students. Ideas: *Generous; ambitious; ingenious; stubborn; frustrated; impatient.*) How did Ishikawa's character change by the end of the story? (Call on different students. Ideas: *He learned discipline and patience; he learned to build kites and became skillful at painting.*) What do you think made Ishikawa's character develop and change in the story? (Call on different students. Idea: *He wanted to steal the golden dolphins so badly that he was willing to do everything that it would take to succeed.*) What parts of Ishikawa's personality stayed the same throughout the story? (Call on different students. Idea: *His determination; ambition; generosity; ingenuity.*)

What kind of person was Katsuta? (Call on different students. Ideas: *Patient, quiet.*) Does Katsuta's character change by the end of the story? (Signal.) *No.* How did Ishikawa treat his teacher Katsuta? (Call on different students. Idea: *With honor and respect.*) What does Ishikawa do or say in the story that shows that he honors and respects Katsuta? (Call on different students. Ideas: *He calls Katsuta "honored one"; he obeyed his teacher's instructions; he tried his painting again after Katsuta silently reproached him for losing his temper.*)

Story Problem

What was Ishikawa's problem at the beginning of the story? (Call on a student. Idea: *He wanted to steal the golden dolphins and sell them to buy rice for the villagers.*) What was the cause of Ishikawa's problem at the beginning of the story? (Call on a student. Idea: *The golden dolphins were on the rooftop of the Shogun's castle, and Ishikawa couldn't think of a way to reach them.*)

What made Ishikawa different from most thieves? (Call on a student. Ideas: *He spent all the gold he stole to buy rice for the hungry people in the villages; he kept only enough money to feed his family.*) What values does Ishikawa have that the Shogun and his son do not? (Call on different students. Idea: *Ishikawa is generous and goodhearted, while the Shogun and his son are greedy and ungenerous for not sharing their fish and their gold with the hungry villagers.*)

Do you think that stealing the golden dolphins was an ambitious and greedy thing to do, or was it a just and heroic action? Justify your point of view. (Call on different students. Accept two or three responses.) What do you think was the author's point of view of the theft? (Call on different students. Idea: *She thought Ishikawa was doing the right thing.*) Are there any clues in the story that tell you that the author thought that Ishikawa's robbery was good? (Call on different students. Idea: *The dragon rescued the prisoners from the boiling oil and brought them to a safe place to live in peace and build kites.*)

Recall your prediction of *The Dragon Kite* before you heard the story. Was your prediction correct? (Call on different students. Accept two or three responses.) Why is the dragon kite grateful, and what reason does he give that Ishikawa should be allowed to live? (Call on a student. Idea: *Ishikawa gave the dragon kite its freedom.*)

What was the effect of Ishikawa's determination to master the art of kite-building? (Call on a student. Idea: *He succeeded in fulfilling his dream.*) Why was Katsuta reluctant to teach Ishikawa the art of kite-building? (Call on a student. Idea: *He said Ishikawa lacks patience, did not know the ways of paper and bamboo, and had no skill with a paintbrush.*) What quality does Ishikawa have that finally convinces the kite-maker to take him on as a student? (Call on a student. Idea: *Determination.*) Raise your hand if you can think of a situation in your life, or in the life of a friend or famous person you admire, where determination led you to succeed in something. (Call on different students. Accept two or three responses.)

How did the new skills and wisdom that Ishikawa's character developed help him cope with the situation when he discovered that the dolphins were too heavy to move? (Call on a student. Idea: *He changed his original plan and tried something different.*) What did the dragon kite remind Ishikawa about when he was discouraged and wanted to give up? (Call on a student. Idea: *To accept what is and try again.*) What solution did Ishikawa come up with? (Call on a student. Idea: *To steal just the dolphins' back and tail fins.*) Sentaro says that the gold was easily gained. What part of the story might make you think that Ishikawa disagrees with this comment? (Call on a student. Idea: *Ishikawa thought of the four years he spent learning how to make kites in Katsuta's shop in order to learn the skills needed to steal the golden dolphins.*)

The **resolution** is often the solution to the problem. What major problem did Ishikawa encounter after he stole the golden dolphin fins? (Call on a student. Ideas: *His friend Sentaro was greedy and betrayed him; he and the kite-maker were imprisoned and were about to be executed.*) Who saved the prisoners? (Signal.) *The dragon kite.*

Theme

The **theme** of a story tells the author's purpose for writing the story. Themes often convey truth and values and provide meaning to the plot of a story.

What do you think is the theme of *The Dragon Kite*? (Call on different students. Ideas: *Determination to follow a dream, and the patience to try again, can make it come true. The heroic deed of robbing from the rich to give to the poor.*) Why do you think the author chose *The Dragon Kite* as the title for her story? (Call on a student. Idea: *It represents all the important values that Ishikawa learned and the fulfillment of a dream.*) Were there any other lessons that you could learn from this folktale and legend? (Call on different students. Ideas: *Nothing comes easily; generosity will be rewarded; patience is invaluable.*)

Language

From what you have read in the story, what do you think a *shogun* is? (Call on a student. Idea: *A rich and powerful ruler or king.*) What parts of the story give you clues about what a *shogun* is? (Call on different students. Ideas: *He is master of all Japan; he built a magnificent castle for his son, with a pair of golden dolphins on the rooftop; he commands many soldiers.*)

When Ishikawa tells his wife that he is going to steal the golden *shachi*, what do you think the Japanese word *shachi* means? (Call on a student. Idea: *Dolphin.*) What word is often used in front of *shachi* that gives you a hint about what this Japanese word means? (Call on a student. Idea: *Golden.*) We are told that the dolphins are golden, so we can deduce that *shachi* means dolphin.

Simile

When a writer uses the words **like** or **as** to compare something to something else, it is called a **simile**. What is it called when a writer uses the words **like** or **as** to compare something to something else? (Signal.) *A simile.*

(Write on the chalkboard: **That tree looks like an alligator. The water was as cold as ice.**) Read the first sentence aloud. (Signal.) *That tree looks like an alligator.* The word **like** compares the way the tree looks to an alligator, so this is a simile. Read the second sentence aloud. (Signal.) *The water was as cold as ice.* The word **as** compares how cold the water was to ice, so this is a simile. Raise your hand if you can make up your own simile using the words **like** or **as** in a comparing sentence. (Call on different students. Accept correct responses.)

(Turn to the page illustrating a red sunset and the thief flying a kite. Read the second paragraph aloud.) Did you hear the words **like** or **as** used in a comparison? (Signal.) *Yes.* The word **like** compares the way Ishikawa's wife's words disappear like fading cherry blossoms in his memory when he thinks about the dolphins, so this is a simile.

(Turn to the next page where Ishikawa attempts to paint a dragon. Read the sentence which begins **His colors were as rippled** . . . that is halfway down the page.) Does this sentence use the words **like** or **as** to make a comparison? (Signal.) *Yes.* To what does the author compare the colors of the paints? (Signal.) *The ripples of a windy sea.*

Metaphor

When one idea is described as being something else to make a comparison, it is called a **metaphor.** What is it called when one idea is described as being something else to make a comparison? (Signal.) *A metaphor.*

(Write on the chalkboard: **Just before she fainted, the walls shimmered in front of her eyes.**) Read the sentence aloud. (Signal.) *Just before she fainted, the walls shimmered in front of her eyes.* Were the walls really shimmering? (Signal.) *No.* This metaphor means that the girl's vision was blurry before she fainted, so the walls seemed to move in wavy lines. Since the walls didn't really shimmer, this word is a metaphor.

(Reread the last sentence of the second paragraph of the page with the sunset aloud.) When the author writes that the dolphins swam endlessly in the wind of Ishikawa's mind, this is a metaphor. Raise your hand if you can explain what the metaphor of the dolphins swimming endlessly in his mind means. (Call on a student. Idea: *Ishikawa thought about the dolphins all the time.*) The dolphins weren't really swimming in Ishikawa's mind, but because he thinks about them so often, it seems that they are always swimming around in his thoughts, so these words are a metaphor.

Summarizing the Literary Analysis

Let's remember some of the things we learned about *The Dragon Kite*, and I'll write them down for you.

What is the purpose of this folktale? (Call on a student. Idea: *To teach a lesson.* Record on chart.)

What are some moral values that are taught in this story? (Call on a student. Idea: *Accept what is and try again.* Record on chart.)

Who are the main characters in this story? (Call on different students. Idea: *Ishikawa and Katsuta.*) What are some character traits of each of these characters? (Call on different students. Ideas: *Ishikawa is stubborn, determined, ambitious, generous; Katsuta is patient, quiet, wise; Sentaro is greedy, disloyal, betrays his friend.*)

What is the theme of the story? (Call on a student. Ideas: *Determination to follow a dream, and the patience to try again, can make it come true. The heroic deed of robbing from the rich to give to the poor.* Record on chart.)

Independent Reading Selection: *Robin Hood* retold by Carol Heyer (English)

ADDITIONAL LITERATURE

Following are some additional titles that your students may enjoy during and following this lesson.

Robin Hood retold by Margaret Early (English)

Any version of *Robin Hood*

Films, audiotapes, or videos that tell the story of *Robin Hood*

Activity

Writing

Title: Response Journal
Time Required: 20 minutes
Materials Required: notebook or journal for each student

1. (Reread the last part of the author's note at the beginning of *The Dragon Kite* aloud.)

2. Legends exaggerate real events from the past. Since somebody did manage to steal the golden dolphins after Ishikawa's attempt, write your own version of a legend about this event from long ago. Remember that the Shogun forbade the building of large kites and encased the golden dolphins in an iron cage. Using your imagination, as well as the information you learned about the dolphins in *The Dragon Kite*, think about how the thief could have stolen these precious statues.

3. Write your ideas for the theft into your notebook as a list, idea web, or brainstorming chart.

4. Now think about the motivation behind this legendary theft. Do you think that the thief's motive was generosity, like Ishikawa's was? What values do you think this thief might have? Will he or she be determined and ingenious like Ishikawa or greedy like the Shogun?

5. (Students could research the real-life events surrounding the theft of the golden dolphins from the roof of Nagoya Castle on the Internet or in computer encyclopedia software in order to base their legends on as much fact as possible.)

Combine each pair of sentences using a conjunction. Use the words **and, but, or, nor, and so**). Rewrite the sentence on the lines below. Remember to use the correct punctuation to introduce the conjunction. On the last line, write a sentence of your own using a conjunction.

1. Xiang wanted to play on the basketball team. The coach said he should try out on Tuesday.

    _____

    _____

2. Helen sprinted down the track with the baton. George grabbed it as quickly as he could.

    _____

    _____

3. Alison didn't have any chocolate icing to frost the cake. She used lemon frosting instead.

    _____

    _____

4. Liam had to finish the decorations. The dance would not take place that weekend.

    _____

    _____

5. Sarah wanted to finish reading her book. It was very late and she felt sleepy.

    _____

    _____

6. _____

    _____

© SRA/McGraw-Hill. Permission is granted to reproduce this page for classroom use.

Lesson 3

Language Skill Development
Using Commas with a Conjunctive Adverb
Time Required: 15 minutes

What is a word that joins two complete sentences called? (Signal.) *A conjunction.* A **conjunctive adverb** is longer than a regular conjunction. It joins two complete sentences, just like a regular conjunction. What is the longer conjunction that joins two complete sentences called? (Signal.) *A conjunctive adverb.* (Write on the chalkboard: **however, besides, instead, therefore, still**. Point to the list of words.) Some conjunctive adverbs that are common are written here. Read the list aloud. (Signal.) *However, besides, instead, therefore, still.*

(Write on the chalkboard: **The clouds appeared dark gray and hung low in the sky. Kenza knew that rain would soon fall.**) Read the first sentence aloud. (Signal.) *The clouds appeared dark gray and hung low in the sky.* Is this a complete sentence? (Signal.) *Yes.* Read the second sentence aloud. (Signal.) *Kenza knew that rain would soon fall.* Is this a complete sentence? (Signal.) *Yes.*

Let's join these two sentences with the conjunctive adverb **therefore**. (Write on the chalkboard: **The clouds appeared dark gray and hung low in the sky therefore Kenza knew that rain would soon fall.**) When you use a conjunctive adverb to join two complete sentences, the conjunctive adverb must have a semicolon before it and a comma after it. What punctuation mark comes before the conjunctive adverb? (Signal.) *A semicolon.* What punctuation mark comes after the conjunctive adverb? (Signal.) *A comma.* (Insert a semicolon before **therefore** and a comma after **therefore**.) Read the sentence aloud. (Signal.) *The clouds appeared dark gray and hung low in the sky; therefore, Kenza knew that rain would soon fall.*

(Write on the chalkboard: **Daniel wanted to ride his bike after school. He had to take out the garbage.**) Read the first sentence aloud. (Signal.) *Daniel wanted to ride his bike after school.* Is this a complete sentence? (Signal.) *Yes.* Read the second sentence aloud. (Signal.) *He had to take out the garbage.* Is this a complete sentence? (Signal.) *Yes.*

Let's join these two sentences with the conjunctive adverb **however**. (Write on the chalkboard: **Daniel wanted to ride his bike after school however he had to take out the garbage first.**) When you use a conjunctive adverb to join two complete sentences, the conjunctive adverb must have a semicolon before it and a comma after it. What punctuation mark comes before the conjunctive adverb? (Signal.) *A semicolon.* What punctuation mark comes after the conjunctive adverb? (Signal.) *A comma.* (Insert a semicolon before **however** and a comma after **however**.) Read the sentence aloud. (Signal.) *Daniel wanted to ride his bike after school; however, he had to take out the garbage first.*

(Write on an overhead transparency, or on the chalkboard: **Driving a car can be fun. It is important to drive safely.**) Now it's your turn. Rewrite this pair of sentences by joining them with the conjunctive adverb **however**. (Write **however** on the chalkboard.) Remember to surround the conjunction with commas.

(Repeat process with the following sentences: **Julian had to go to the dentist. He missed a morning of school.** [therefore] **Joon-Hi wanted to play softball. She decided to try out for track and field.** [however])

Literature

Androcles and the Lion

by Dennis Nolan

Materials required: A map of the world
Folk Literature Summary Chart started in Lesson 1

> **Note:** After a class discussion of the selected book, an independent reading option of a second book is recommended. The books listed follow similar plot, characterization, and themes. You may wish to have your students read the recommended book independently (or in pairs or groups) and compare and contrast the optional selection by modeling their chart summaries (BLM 1B) on the chart completed during class discussion.

Let's review the four purposes for folk literature. The first purpose for folk literature is: (Signal. Hold up one finger for each purpose.) *To tell about the creation of the world.* The second purpose is: (Signal.) *To explain how things came to be.* The third purpose is: (Signal.) *To entertain.* And the fourth purpose is: (Signal.) *To teach a lesson.* (Repeat until firm.)

Examining the Book

This is the next book that we are going to read and discuss. (Point to the title.) Read the title of the book. (Signal.) *Androcles and the Lion.* (Record on class chart. Point to the author's name on the cover.) Who is the author of this book? (Call on a student. *Dennis Nolan.* Record on class chart. Point to the illustrator's name on the cover.) Who is the illustrator of *Androcles and the Lion*? (Call on a student. *Dennis Nolan.*)

Today's story is Roman. The city of Rome is in the country of Italy. (Show students the location of Rome on a world map.) During the time when this story takes place, Rome controlled an empire so vast that it stretched all the way to England. What is the origin of this story? (Signal.) *Rome.* (Record on class chart.) The original story of *Androcles and the Lion* was written by an Egyptian named Apion around 40 A.D. Apion witnessed the events in the story himself, then wrote the story based on what he saw. There are several different versions of this Roman story, but Dennis Nolan wrote the version that we will read today.

The genre of *Androcles and the Lion* is a fable. What genre is *Androcles and the Lion*? (Signal.) *A fable.* (Record on chart.) A fable is a short story that teaches a lesson about human nature. What is a fable? (Signal.) *A short story that teaches a lesson about human nature.*

The genre of *Androcles and the Lion* is a legend as well, because the story is based on a real event that happened a long time ago. What other genre is *Androcles and the Lion*? (Signal.) *A legend.* (Record on chart.) A legend often exaggerates real events or people. What is a legend? (Signal.) *A story that exaggerates real events or people.*

Making Predictions

Androcles and the Lion is a fable and legend that takes place in Rome, was written by an Egyptian named Apion around 40 A.D., and is based on an eyewitness event. Raise your hand if you can make a prediction about what will happen in this story. Tell about the event Apion might have witnessed, what trouble you think the character will get into, and how he gets out of trouble. (Call on different students. Accept two or three responses.)

(Show students the front cover of the book.) Raise your hand if you would like to predict what is happening in the part of the story that the cover illustrates. Tell us what part of the illustration gives you an idea about what is happening. (Call on different students. Accept two or three responses.)

What do you think is the relationship between Androcles and the lion, based on the front cover illustration? (Call on different students. Accept two or three responses.)

Predict the purpose of this fable, based on what you already know about the story. Do you think it will be a creation myth, an explaining story, a trickster tale to entertain, or a story that teaches a lesson? Give a reason to support your prediction. (Call on different students. Accept reasonable responses.)

Reading the Book

Choose one of the two options presented in Lesson 1 for reading the book. If students read parts of the story aloud remind them of the conventions for being an effective speaker and listener found in Lesson 1.

Occasionally, you may find it beneficial to discuss parts of the story that are complicated or that have unfamiliar vocabulary. Encourage students to check the illustrations, the structures of words, and context to help them decipher unknown words and their meanings.)

Literary Analysis

(Read the author's note at the back of the book aloud.) Where was Apion when he saw a lion spare a slave's life? (Call on a student. Idea: *The Circus Maximus.*) Apion made up a story about why he thought the lion and the slave were friends. What do you think might have been the reason that the lion didn't kill the slave? (Call on different students. Accept two or three responses.)

Let's talk about the setting of this fable. Where does this story happen? (Call on a student. Ideas: *On the edge of the Egyptian desert; in the Roman Empire.* Show students the location of Egypt on a world map.) When does this story happen? (Call on a student. Idea: *Long ago.*)

Is there anything in the illustrations or the story itself that tells you about the landscape, people, clothing, or culture of the Roman Empire and Egypt in the ancient time that this fable takes place? (Call on different students. Ideas: *Short sleeveless tunics; desert; hot weather; Androcles is barefoot and there is a boiling sun; Roman armor; horses and chariots; slaves; an emperor; unique names; wild animals killing people for entertainment.*)

Think about the next three questions that I am going to ask. Do you think that these things might still be important to the culture of Rome today? What do you think might have changed? What might have stayed the same? (Call on different students. Ideas: *The weather is probably still hot, there is still a desert in Egypt; no slaves or emperors; cars instead of chariots; people probably wear modern clothes; no people killed for fun by wild animals.*)

Why do you think that the Romans stopped having arenas where people were killed for entertainment? (Call on different students. Idea: *It wasn't considered socially acceptable to kill humans for sport.*) In what way do you think that values have changed since ancient times? (Call on different students. Accept two or three responses.)

Who are the main characters in *Androcles and the Lion*? (Call on different students. Ideas: *Androcles; his master; the lion.*) What kind of person was Androcles at the beginning of the story? (Call on different students. Ideas: *Unhappy; brave; determined; kind; enslaved.*) How did Androcles's character change by the end of the story? (Call on different students. Ideas: *He became happy; free; laughing; triumphant. He was a free man.*) What do you think made Androcles' character develop and change in the story? (Call on different students. Ideas: *He was determined to improve his life by escaping from slavery; he made a best friend.*) What parts of Androcles' personality stayed the same throughout the story? (Call on different students. Idea: *His kindness, his friendship with the lion.*)

What kind of person was Androcles' master? (Call on different students. Ideas: *Cruel, angry, bossy.*) Does the master's character change by the end of the story? (Signal.) *No.* How did Androcles treat the hurt lion? (Call on different students. Idea: *Gently and helpfully.*) What does Androcles do or say in the story that shows that he is a kind man? (Call on different students. Ideas: *He feels sorry for the lion and tells it not to worry. He heals the lion by pulling the thorn out of its paw.*) How did the lion treat Androcles? (Call on different students. Ideas: *Kindly; gratefully; with friendliness.*)

How does their friendship make life better for both of them before the soldiers arrive? (Call on different students. Ideas: *The lion brought Androcles food; Androcles brought the lion companionship.*) How does their friendship save them both after they are captured by the soldiers? (Call on different students. Ideas: *The lion spares Androcles' life; Androcles frees himself and the captured lion by telling the emperor and the people the story of their friendship.*)

Story Problem

What was Androcles' problem at the beginning of the story? (Call on a student. Idea: *He was enslaved by a cruel master.*) What was the cause of Androcles' problem at the beginning of the story? (Call on a student. Idea: *His cruel master.*)

What did Androcles decide to do to solve his problem? (Call on a student. Idea: *Risk death by running away.*) What values does Androcles have that his master does not? (Call on different students. Ideas: *Androcles is kind, his master is cruel; Androcles wants to heal the lion, his master wants to whip Androcles; Androcles is helpful and friendly, his master is angry and hateful.*)

The resolution is often the solution to the problem. Why do you think that the arena audience voted to save Androcles and the lion? (Call on a student. Ideas: *They thought Androcles did a kind and heroic thing by helping the lion. They felt sorry for him.*) What values do you think the audience approved of and valued in Androcles and the lion? (Call on different students. Ideas: *Kindness; strong friendship; the gratefulness of the lion.*)

Recall what you predicted that Apion witnessed before you heard the story. Was your prediction correct? (Call on different students. Accept two or three responses.)

Theme

The theme of a story tells the author's purpose for writing the story. Themes often convey truth and values and provide meaning to the plot of a story.

What do you think is the theme of *Androcles and the Lion*? (Call on different students. Idea: *Kindness and compassion for others is often repaid.*) Why do you think so many authors, from Apion to Dennis Nolan, chose to write about the story of Androcles and the lion? (Call on different students. Idea: *It is an exciting story that teaches about kindness, friendship, and gratitude.*)

Sensory Language

Authors often use language that helps readers feel like they are taking part in the action of the story. Words that help readers feel, see, smell, taste, and hear events are called **sensory language.** What is sensory language? (Signal.) *Words that help readers feel, see, smell, taste, and hear events.*

(Write on the chalkboard: **Rudy crunched her cereal and slurped her milk.**) Read the sentence aloud. (Signal.) *Rudy crunched her cereal and slurped her milk.* Raise your hand if you can tell us which words help you hear what Rudy is doing as though you were in the room with her. (Call on a student. Idea: *Crunched, slurped.*) **Crunched** and **slurped** are examples of sensory language.

(Turn to the page where Androcles runs away from his master. Read the first sentence of the last paragraph aloud.) How do you know if the night is very dark or brightly lit? (Call on a student. Idea: *It was a moonless night, so it was very dark.*) What words tell you if Androcles rustled and stomped out of the house, or if he tried to be very quiet? (Call on different students. Ideas: *He slipped away; he crept silently.*)

(Turn to the page where Androcles steps inside the lion's cave. Read the first two sentences aloud.) What is the floor like? (Call on a student. Idea: *Cool, hard.*) How do Androcles feet feel? (Signal.) *Burning.* How does the floor feel on Androcles's feet? (Call on a student. Idea: *Soothing and cool.*)

Summarizing the Literary Analysis

Let's remember some of the things we learned about *Androcles and the Lion*, and I'll write them down for you.

What is the purpose of this fable? (Call on a student. Idea: *To teach a lesson.* Record on chart.)

What moral value is taught in this story? (Call on a student. Idea: *Kindness is often rewarded with gratitude.* Record on chart.)

Who are the main characters in this story? (Call on different students. Ideas: *Androcles, the lion, Androcles's master.*) What are some character traits of each of these characters? (Call on different students. Ideas: *Androcles is kind and helpful; his master is cruel and angry; the lion is friendly and grateful.*)

What is the theme of the story? (Call on a student. Idea: *Kindness and compassion for others is often repaid.* Record on chart.) The theme of a fable is called the **moral.** What is the theme of a fable called? (Signal.) *A moral.*

Independent Reading Selection: *Aesop's Fables* illustrated by Jerry Pinkney

Any version of *Aesop's Fables*

ADDITIONAL LITERATURE

Following are some additional titles that your students may enjoy during and following this lesson.

Any version of *Androcles and the Lion*

Films, audiotapes, or videos that tell the story of *Androcles and the Lion*

Activity

Speaking/Writing

Title: Response Journal

Time Required: 20 minutes

Materials Required: notebook or journal for each student

1. Fables teach a lesson using important human values. Usually, one or more characters in a fable is an animal. Animals in fables often have certain characteristics that help storytellers teach their lesson. For example, lions are fierce and brave, rabbits are quick, turtles are slow, elephants have good memories, eagles are proud. Raise your hand if you can think of an animal that has a characteristic that demonstrates a human character trait. **(Call on different students. Accept two or three responses.)**

2. Think about a human value that you think is important. This can be a moral or a lesson about human relationships. Write your ideas for a moral at the top of a page in your notebook. Decide on an animal that has a characteristic that will help you explain or demonstrate the moral of your choice.

3. Now think about the story *Androcles and the Lion*. Rewrite the fable using a new moral and the animal that you selected in place of the lion and the moral of kindness being repaid.

4. Will the audience in your fable think that Androcles and your new animal should be saved because of the human values they represent, or will your character be punished for running away from his or her master?

5. Include as much sensory language in your fable as you can. Try to make your readers hear, feel, smell, taste, and see the action as though they were really there while the story is being told.

Lesson 4

Language Skill Development

Listening/Speaking/Writing

> **Title: Homonyms**
> **Time Required:** 20 minutes
> **Materials Required:** BLM 4A, one copy for each student

When two words sound exactly the same, but have different meanings, they're called homonyms. What are two words that sound exactly the same, but have different meanings called? (Signal.) *Homonyms.*

(Write on the chalkboard: **see, sea.**) Read these two words aloud. (Signal.) *See, sea.* Raise your hand if you can tell us what the first word means. (Call on a student. Idea: *To look at something.*) Raise your hand if you can tell us what the second word means. (Call on a student. Idea: *The ocean.*) Do both words sound exactly the same? (Signal.) *Yes.* Do they mean the same thing? (Signal.) *No.* **See** and **sea** are homonyms.

(Write on the chalkboard: **blew, blue**.) Read these two words aloud. (Signal.) *Blew, blue.* Raise your hand if you can tell us what the first word means. (Call on a student. Idea: *Puffed air.*) Raise your hand if you can tell us what the second word means. (Call on a student. Idea: *A color.*) Do both words sound exactly the same? (Signal.) *Yes.* Do they mean the same thing? (Signal.) *No.* **Blew** and **blue** are homonyms.

Raise your hand if you can think of another pair of homonyms. (Call on different students. Ideas: *Wait, weight; right, write, rite, wright; by, buy, bye; hear, here.* Write correct responses on the chalkboard.)

When you proofread your work for spelling it is important to check for homonyms. You must read how the word is used in the sentence to determine how it is spelled. The meaning of the word will help you decide which spelling to use.

(Pass out BLM 4A to each student.) Read each sentence carefully. Then decide which of the homonyms in brackets is correct. Then, write the correct homonym on the line provided.

Literature

Pedro and the Monkey

by Robert D. San Souci

Materials required: A map of the world
Folk Literature Summary Chart started in Lesson 1

> **Note:** After a class discussion of the selected book, an independent reading option of a second book is recommended. The books listed follow similar plot, characterization, and themes. You may wish to have your students read the recommended book independently (or in pairs or groups) and compare and contrast the optional selection by modeling their chart summaries (BLM 1B) on the chart completed during class discussion. At the end of each literature lesson, you will find a cross-cultural list of additional books or stories with similar plots and themes that may be used as supplementary reading for each literature lesson.

Many folktales are told for a purpose. Let's review the four purposes for folk literature. The first purpose for folk literature is: (Signal. Hold up one finger for each purpose.) *To tell about the creation of the world.* The second purpose is: (Signal.) *To explain how things came to be.* The third purpose is: (Signal.) *To entertain.* And the fourth purpose is: (Signal.) *To teach a lesson.* (Repeat until firm.)

Examining the Book

This is the next book that we are going to read and discuss. (Point to the title.) Read the title of the book. (Signal.) *Pedro and the Monkey.* (Record on class chart. Point to the author's name on the cover.) Who is the author of this book? (Call on a student. *Robert D. San Souci.* Record on class chart. Point to the illustrator's name on the cover.) Who is the illustrator of *Pedro and the Monkey*? (Call on a student. *Michael Hays.)*

Today's story is from the Philippines. (Show students the location of the Philippines on a world map.) Where is the origin of this story? (Signal.) *The Philippines.* (Record on class chart.)

The genre of *Pedro and the Monkey* is a folktale. What genre is *Pedro and the Monkey*? (Signal.) *A folktale.* (Record on chart.) What is a folktale? (Signal.) *A story that has been told by people for a long time.*

Making Predictions

(Show students the front cover of the book.) Raise your hand if you would like to predict what is happening in the part of the story that the cover illustrates. Tell us what part of the illustration gives you an idea about what is happening. (Call on different students. Accept two or three responses.)

What do you think the relationship between Pedro and the monkey is based on the front cover illustration? (Call on different students. Accept two or three responses.)

Monkeys are very clever animals. Keeping this in mind, predict the purpose of this folktale, based on what you already know about the story. Do you think it will be a creation myth, an explaining story, a trickster tale to entertain, or a story that teaches a lesson? Give a reason to support your prediction. (Call on different students. Accept reasonable responses.)

Reading the Book

Choose one of the two options presented in lesson one for reading the book. If students read parts of the story aloud remind them of the conventions for being an effective speaker and listener found in Lesson 1.

Occasionally, you may find it beneficial to discuss parts of the story that are complicated or that have unfamiliar vocabulary. Encourage students to check the illustrations, the structures of words, and context to help them decipher unknown words and their meanings.)

Literary Analysis

Let's talk about the setting of this folktale. Where does this story happen? (Call on a student. Ideas: *On the farm of a young Filipino farmer; the Philippines.*) When does this folktale happen? (Call on a student. Idea: *Long ago.*)

Is there anything in the illustrations or the story itself that tells you about the landscape, clothing, people, or Filipino culture in the time that this folktale takes place? (Call on different students. Ideas: *The unique names of the characters; sunshine and blue skies; palm trees; monkeys; cool, white clothes; dark hair; geometrical patterns and designs; gold coins.*)

Think about the next three questions that I am going to ask. Do you think that these things might still be important in Filipino culture today? What do you think might have changed? What might have stayed the same? (Call on different students. Ideas: *The weather is probably still warm and sunny; there are probably still palm trees and monkeys; the geometrical designs might still be popular; people might still wear cool clothing but in modern fashions; they don't use gold coins anymore.*)

Who are the main characters in *Pedro and the Monkey*? (Call on different students. Idea: *Pedro, the monkey, Don Francisco.*) What kind of person was Pedro at the beginning of the story? (Call on different students. Ideas: *He had a generous heart; kind; worried by the monkey's tricks.*) Do you think that Pedro's character changed in any way by the end of the story? (Call on different students. Idea: *No.*)

Pedro started out very poor and ended up the rich owner of a magnificent house, large fields, and huge estate. Do you predict that all this wealth will change Pedro's personality, or will he keep his generous heart and kind nature? Use what you learned about Pedro from the story to back up your answers. (Call on different students. Accept two or three responses.)

What kind of animal was the monkey? (Call on different students. Ideas: *Smart; cunning; tricky; sneaky; grateful to Pedro for not selling him; has good manners; bold; brave.*) What does the monkey do in the story that shows you that he is smart and tricky? (Call on different students. Ideas: *He makes Don Francisco think that Pedro is very rich and owns a magnificent house; he makes the merchant believe that Pedro is the richest man in the world; he makes Burincantada think that there is a Giant-Eater after him.*)

Think about the purpose you predicted for this story before you heard it. Now that you know about all the tricky and sneaky things the monkey does, do you want to change your mind about what the purpose of this folktale is, or was your prediction accurate? (Call on different students. Accept two or three responses.)

Trickster tales often exaggerate the cleverness or the stupidity of the animal characters. Does this apply to the monkey in this folktale? (Signal.) *Yes.* Often, the animals in trickster tales act very much like humans. Does the monkey act like a human in *Pedro and the Monkey*? How? (Call on different students. Ideas: *He talks; he is smarter than all the human characters; he wears clothes; he has good manners and is charming; he eats at the table with a spoon.*)

Story Problem

What was Pedro's problem at the very beginning of the story? (Call on a student. Idea: *A monkey was stealing his corn.*) What was the cause of Pedro's problem at the beginning of the story? (Call on a student. Idea: *The monkey.*)

What did Pedro decide to do to solve his problem? (Call on a student. Idea: *Set a trap to catch the monkey.*) The monkey persuaded Pedro to let him go by appealing to Pedro's emotions and his soft heart, but also by using logical arguments. (Reread aloud the section of the first page where the monkey persuaded Pedro to free him.) What language in the story tells you that the monkey is using an emotional argument? (Call on a student. Idea: *By bursting into tears and begging.*) What language in the story tells you that the monkey is using a logical argument? (Call on a student. Idea: *He promises not to steal any more corn.*)

Raise your hand if you can think of other times when the monkey used persuasive language to convince a character that his tricks were the truth. (Call on different students. Ideas: *He flatters Burincantada and convinces him that a Giant-Eater is coming; he bows and charms and impresses Don Francisco with good manners and lies.*)

The monkey wants to repay Pedro for his kindness. What new problems does the monkey create for Pedro with his tricks and his lies? (Call on different students. Ideas: *The monkey gives Don Francisco his last three centavos; Pedro is worried Don Francisco will think he stole the gold coins; Pedro is invited to dinner but doesn't have any nice clothes to wear; he falls in love with Maria, but can't have them visit his poor hut.*)

Do you think that the part of the story where the monkey convinces the clothes merchant that Pedro is the richest man in the world is believable? (Call on a student. Idea: *No.*) Do you think that a merchant could really be tricked that easily? (Call on different students. Idea: *No, the clothes merchant is too gullible.*) What could the monkey have shown the merchant or said or done in the story to more realistically trick the clothes merchant? (Call on different students. Ideas: *He could have said Pedro was a good friend of Don Francisco; the monkey could have brought a scrap of fine cloth and said it ripped off Pedro's shirt; he could have described Pedro's imaginary wealth.* Accept reasonable responses.)

Let's discuss the resolution of the story. The monkey repaid Pedro's goodness by making him a rich and happy man. Who else benefited from Pedro's kindness to the monkey by the end of the story? (Call on different students. Ideas: *Don Francisco found a good husband for his daughter. Maria fell in love with Pedro and they lived happily. The prisoners in the mansion were set free. Burincantada was punished for eating people and keeping prisoners.*) Would you have predicted that such a small gesture of kindness could have had so many good effects? (Call on a student. Idea: *No.*)

Theme

What do you think the theme of *Pedro and the Monkey* is? (Call on different students. Idea: *Kindness and compassion for others is often repaid.*)

Idiomatic Language

When you use words that everyone knows the meaning of, but that aren't really true to explain something, it's called an **idiomatic expression.** What's it called when you use words that aren't really true to explain something? (Signal.) *An idiomatic expression.*

(Write on the chalkboard: **Louis spilled the beans about the surprise party. Donna was angry that Louis had let the cat out of the bag**.) Read the first sentence. (Signal.) *Louis spilled the beans about the surprise party.* Did Louis really spill some beans? (Signal.) *No.* Raise your hand if you can explain what the idiomatic expression of spilling the beans means. (Call on a student. Idea: *Telling information that is supposed to be a secret.*)

Read the second sentence. (Signal.) *Donna was angry that Louis had let the cat out of the bag.* Did Louis let a real cat out of a bag? (Signal.) *No.* Raise your hand if you can explain what the idiomatic expression of letting the cat out of the bag means. (Call on a student. Idea: *Telling information that is supposed to be a secret.*)

(Turn to the page where Pedro and Maria fall in love. Read the two last sentences aloud.) Do you think Pedro and Maria's eyeballs were literally on each other? (Signal.) *No.* Raise your hand if you can explain what the idiomatic expression "could not keep their eyes off each other" means. (Call on a student. Idea: *They kept looking at each other.*)

(Turn to the next page. Read the first sentence aloud.) Do you think that Pedro and his emotions were carried away to some other place? (Signal.) *No.* Raise your hand if you can explain what the idiomatic expression "was carried away with emotion" means. (Call on a student. Idea: *Pedro was so in love with Maria that he acted in an unusual and outgoing way.*)

Language

From what you have read in the story, what do you think a *bubog* tree looks like? (Call on a student. Idea: *A shady tree with branches that spread like an umbrella.*) What parts of the story give you clues about what a *bubog* tree looks like? (Call on different students. Ideas: *The descriptive language; the illustrations.*)

When the monkey asks to borrow a *ganta*, how do you know what this is? (Call on a student. Idea: *In the story, it is used to measure rice, so it is a special-sized measurement. The illustrations show that it is a wooden box about a foot wide.*) What word is often used after *ganta* that gives you a hint about what this Filipino word means? (Call on a student. Idea: *Measure.*) We are told that the *ganta* is used as a measure, so we can deduce that *ganta* means a kind of measurement.

The monkey wants Pedro's last three *centavos*. This word is used so often that you probably know what it means. Raise your hand if you can tell us what *centavos* are. (Call on a student. Idea: *Coins.*) Do you think that three centavos are worth the same amount back when this story is told as they are now? (Signal.) *No.* For Pedro, three centavos was a lot of money.

(Reread the passage where the monkey flatters the giant aloud.) When the giant snatches up a handful of *carabao* to eat, how do you know what *carabao* are? (Call on a student. Idea: *In the story, the author tells us that they are a kind of water buffalo.*) If the giant snatches up handfuls of *carabao,* can you infer that these buffalo graze alone or in herds? (Signal.) *In herds.*

Summarizing the Literary Analysis

Let's remember some of the things we learned about *Pedro and the Monkey*, and I'll write them down for you.

What is the purpose of this folktale? (Call on a student. Idea: *A trickster tale, to entertain.* Record on chart.)

What moral value is taught in this story? (Call on a student. Idea: *Kindness is often rewarded with gratitude.* Record on chart.)

Who are the main characters in this story? (Call on different students. Ideas: *Pedro; the monkey; Don Francisco.*) What are some character traits of each of these characters? (Call on different students. Ideas: *Pedro has a good heart and is kind; the monkey is grateful, smart, tricky, sneaky, and bold; Don Francisco is amazed, confused, suspicious, awed.*)

What is the theme of the story? (Call on a student. Idea: *Kindness and compassion for others is often repaid.* Record on chart.)

Independent Reading Selection: *Puss in Boots* by Charles Perrault, illustrated by Fred Marcellino.

ADDITIONAL LITERATURE

Following are some additional titles that your students may enjoy during and following this lesson.

Any version of *Puss in Boots*

Films, audiotapes, or videos that tell the story of *Puss in Boots*

Activity

Writing

> ### Title: Making a Comparison Chart
>
> **Time Required:** 30 minutes
>
> **Materials Required:** BLM 4B, one copy for each student; as many copies of *Puss in Boots* as possible for students to share (you may use different versions of *Puss in Boots*)
>
> **Preparation:** Copy the three Venn Diagrams from the BLM onto an overhead transparency or the chalkboard:

Procedure

1. (Ensure that all students have read a copy of *Puss in Boots*.)

2. There are many parallels between the plot, setting, and characterization of *Pedro and the Monkey* and *Puss in Boots*. (Point to the plot diagrams.) In the left circle, write a short plot summary in point form for *Pedro and the Monkey*. In the right circle, write a short plot summary for *Puss in Boots*. In the center where the two circles overlap, write how the plots of the two stories are the same.

3. Working independently, in pairs, or in a group, write down notes about the setting of *Pedro and the Monkey* in the left circle of the setting diagram. Write notes about the setting of *Puss in Boots* in the right circle. In the center where the two circles overlap, write how the settings of the two stories are the same.

4. In the characterization diagram, write who the main characters are in *Pedro and the Monkey*, and a short summary of their personalities in the left circle. In the right circle, write who the main characters are in *Puss in Boots*. Add a short summary of their personalities. In the center where the two circles overlap, write how the characters in the two stories are similar and behave similarly.

Read each sentence carefully. Decide which of the homonyms in brackets is correct. Then, write the correct homonym on the line provided. You may use a dictionary to help you decide which spelling is correct.

1. Tell Roberto to _____ (meat, meet) us at the park.

2. The nurse put a blanket made of _____ (led, lead) over the x-ray patient.

3. (Hour, Our) _____ clock rang every (hour, our) _____.

4. Sophia _____ (led, lead) her horse over the bridge.

5. Please ask the mechanic to look at the front _____ (brake, break).

6. _____ (You're, Your) going shopping with _____ (you're, your) friends on Friday.

7. Dave didn't _____ (brake, break) the jug; I did.

8. Mr. Jordan said it was a _____ (fare, fair) price for the stereo.

9. Sumiko brought just enough money to pay the bus _____ (fare, fair).

10. The _____ (bare, bear) gorged itself on honey.

© SRA/McGraw-Hill. Permission is granted to reproduce this page for classroom use.

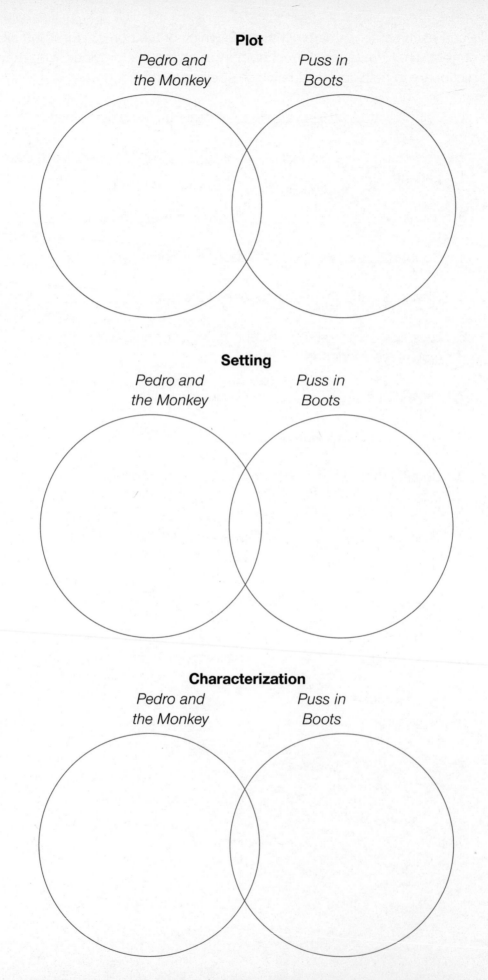

Plot

*Pedro and
the Monkey*   *Puss in
Boots*

Setting

*Pedro and
the Monkey*   *Puss in
Boots*

Characterization

*Pedro and
the Monkey*   *Puss in
Boots*

© SRA/McGraw-Hill. Permission is granted to reproduce this page for classroom use.

Lesson 5

Language Skill Development

Commonly Misspelled Homonyms

Time Required: 20 minutes
Materials Required: BLM 5 for each student

When two or more words sound exactly the same but have different meanings, they're called **homonyms.** What are words called that sound exactly the same but have different meanings called? (Signal.) *Homonyms.*

(Write on the chalkboard: **to, too, two.**) Read these three words aloud. (Signal.) *To, too, two.* Raise your hand if you can tell us what the first word means. (Call on a student. Idea: *Going to a thing or place.*) Raise your hand if you can tell us what the second word means. (Call on a student. Ideas: *Also; as well as.*) Raise your hand if you can tell us what the third word means. (Call on a student. Idea: *The number that comes between one and three.*) Do all three words sound exactly the same? (Signal.) *Yes.* Do they mean the same thing? (Signal.) *No.* **To, too,** and **two** are homonyms that are often difficult to spell correctly unless you check for their meaning in a sentence.

(Write on the chalkboard: **We are going _____ Julia's party next Friday.**) Read the sentence aloud. (Signal.) *We are going blank Julia's party next Friday.* (Write on the chalkboard: **to, too, two.** Point to **two**.) **Two** spelled **t-w-o** is a number. Does putting a number in this sentence make sense? (Signal.) *No.* (Cross out **two.**)

(Point to **too.**) **Too** spelled **t-o-o** means the same thing as **also.** Let's substitute **also** for the blank and read the sentence aloud to see if it makes sense. Read the sentence aloud with **also.** (Signal.) *We are going also Julia's party next Friday.* Does this make sense? (Signal.) *No.* (Cross out too.)

(Point to **to.**) **To** spelled **t-o** means going to a place or thing. (Underline **Julia's party.**) Is a party a place or a thing? (Signal.) *Yes.* (Insert **to** into the blank on the chalkboard.) Read the sentence aloud. (Signal.) *We are going to Julia's party next Friday.* Does this make sense? (Signal.) *Yes.*

(Write on the chalkboard: **Can Daniel and Melissa come _____?** Repeat above process.)

(Write on the chalkboard: **there, their, they're.**) Read these three words aloud. (Signal.) *There, their, they're.* Raise your hand if you can tell us what the first word means. (Call on a student. Idea: *A place where something is.*) Raise your hand if you can tell us what the second word means. (Call on a student. Idea: *Belonging to two or more people.*) Raise your hand if you can tell us what the third word means. (Call on a student. Idea: *They are.*) Do all three words sound exactly the same? (Signal.) *Yes.* Do they mean the same thing? (Signal.) *No.* **There, their,** and **they're** are homonyms that are often tricky to get right.

(Write on the chalkboard: **_____ ball rolled over _____ by the grass.**) Read the sentence aloud. (Signal.) *Blank ball rolled over blank by the grass.* (Write on the chalkboard: **there, their, they're.** Point to **they're.**) **They're** spelled **t-h-e-y-apostrophe-r-e** is a contraction for **they are.** Let's substitute **they are** in both blanks and see if it makes sense. Read the sentence aloud substituting **they are** for the blanks. (Signal.) *They are ball rolled over they are by the grass.* Does putting **they are** in this sentence make sense? (Signal.) *No.* (Cross out **they're.**)

(Point to **their.**) **Their** spelled **t-h-e-i-r** means belonging to two or more people. Could the ball belong to some people? (Signal.) *Yes.* (Write **their** in the first blank. Point to **there.**) **There** spelled **t-h-e-r-e** means a place where something is. Is by the grass a place? (Signal.) *Yes.* (Write **there** in the second blank.) Now read the sentence aloud. (Signal.) *Their ball rolled over there by the grass.* Does this make sense? (Signal.) *Yes.*

(Pass out BLM 5 to each student.) Read each sentence carefully. Then decide which of the homonyms in brackets is correct. Then write the correct homonym on the line provided.

Literature

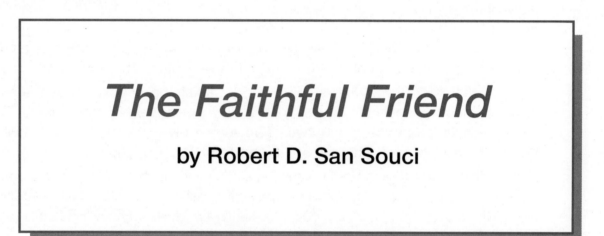

The Faithful Friend

by Robert D. San Souci

Materials required: A map of the world
Folk Literature Summary Chart started in Lesson 1

> **Note:** After a class discussion of the selected book, an independent reading option of a second book is recommended. The books listed follow similar plot, characterization, and themes. You may wish to have your students read the recommended book independently (or in pairs or groups) and compare and contrast the optional selection by modeling their chart summaries (BLM 1B) on the chart completed during class discussion.

Many folktales are told for a purpose. Let's review the four purposes for folk literature. The first purpose for folk literature is: (Signal. Hold up one finger for each purpose.) *To tell about the creation of the world.* The second purpose is: (Signal.) *To explain how things came to be.* The third purpose is: (Signal.) *To entertain.* And the fourth purpose is: (Signal.) *To teach a lesson.* (Repeat until firm.)

Examining the Book

This is the next book that we are going to read and discuss. (Point to the title.) Read the title of the book. (Signal.) *The Faithful Friend.* (Record on class chart. Point to the author's name on the cover.) Who is the author of this book? (Call on a student. *Robert D. San Souci.* Point to the illustrator's name on the cover.) Who is the illustrator of *The Faithful Friend*? (Call on a student. *Brian Pinkney.*)

Today's story is from the French West Indies. (Show students the location of the French West Indies on a world map.) Where is the origin of this story? (Signal.) *The French West Indies.* (Record on class chart.)

The genre of *The Faithful Friend* is a folktale. What genre is *The Faithful Friend*? (Signal.) *A folktale.* (Record on chart.) What is a folktale? (Signal.) *A story that has been told by people for a long time.*

Making Predictions

(Open the front and back covers of the book so that students see the picture in its entirety.) Raise your hand if you would like to predict what is happening in the part of the story that the cover illustrates. Tell us what part of the illustration gives you an idea about what is happening. (Call on different students. Accept two or three responses.)

What do you think is the relationship between the two boys, based on the cover illustration? (Call on different students. Accept one or two responses.)

Keeping the title of this folktale in mind, predict its purpose. Do you think it will be a creation myth, an explaining story, a trickster tale to entertain, or a story that teaches a lesson? Give a reason to support your prediction. (Call on different students. Accept reasonable responses.)

Reading the Book

Choose one of the two options presented in Lesson 1 for reading the book. If students read parts of the story aloud, remind them of the conventions for being an effective speaker and listener found in Lesson 1.

Occasionally, you may find it beneficial to discuss parts of the story that are complicated or that have unfamiliar vocabulary. Encourage students to check the illustrations, the structure of words, and context to help them decipher unknown words and their meanings.)

Literary Analysis

Let's talk about the setting of this folktale. Where does this story happen? (Call on a student. Idea: *On the island of Martinique in the Caribbean Sea.*) When does this folktale happen? (Call on a student. Idea: *In the last century.*)

(Show students the illustrations and read the last paragraph of the second page that describes the setting aloud.) Is there anything in the illustrations or the story itself that tells you about the landscape, people, or culture of the French West Indies in the time period that this folktale takes place? (Call on different students. Ideas: *The unique* names of the characters; the names of the towns; the plantations; hot sun and blue skies; palm trees; vivid blossoms; sugarcane; pineapple; banana; mango; lemon and lime fields; distant mountains; the ocean; French greetings.)

Raise your hand if you can tell us how the setting affects the moods of the two young men. (Call on a student. Ideas: *The vivid blossoms and beautiful view of the mountains was a perfect setting for their high spirits; they were in a joyful mood.*) Why did the boys walk slowly? (Call on a student. Idea: *Because the sun was very hot.*)

Who are the main characters in *The Faithful Friend*? (Call on different students. Idea: *Clement; Hippolyte; Pauline; Monsieur Zabocat.*) What kind of person was Clement at the beginning of the story? (Call on different students. Ideas: *He was high-spirited; in love; happy; friendly with Hippolyte.*) Do you think that Clement's character changed in any way by the end of the story? (Call on different students. Ideas: *He became angry with Hippolyte, worried, sad.*) What happened that changed Clement's character? (Call on a student. Ideas: *He thought that Hippolyte wanted to kill him. His best friend turned to stone.*) How did Clement's character stay the same? (Call on different students. Idea: *He renewed his friendship and loyalty to Hippolyte by offering to change himself into stone instead.*)

What kind of person was Hippolyte? Use an example from the story to back up your idea. (Call on different students. Ideas: *Loyal, because he saved his friend from the zombies; cautious, because he warned Clement not to rely just on a picture of a girl; troubled, because the forest was strangely silent and he heard drums.*)

What kind of person was Pauline? Use an example from the story to back up your idea. (Call on different students. Ideas: *Cheerful, because of her bright smile and her talk and laughter with Clement; lively and spirited, because she stood up to her uncle, witty.*)

What kind of person was Monsieur Zabocat? Use an example from the story to back up your idea. (Call on different students. Ideas: *Furious when Pauline agreed to marry Clement; protective because he forbids the marriage; evil because he sends three zombies to kill the three friends.*)

Think about the purpose you predicted for this story before you heard it. Do you want to change your mind about what the purpose of this folktale is, or was your prediction accurate? (Call on different students. Accept two or three responses.)

Story Problem

What was the main characters' problem after Pauline left her uncle to go with Clement? (Call on a student. Idea: *Monsieur Zabocat asked three zombie women to kill them.*) What was the cause of their problem? (Call on a student. Ideas: *Monsieur Zabocat; the zombies.*)

Did all the main characters know about the problem? (Signal.) *No.* Who knew about the problem and who didn't? (Call on different students. Idea: *Clement and Pauline didn't know they were in danger; only Hippolyte and Monsieur Zabocat knew.*) Why couldn't Hippolyte warn his friend of their danger? (Call on a student. Idea: *Because he would have been turned to stone.*)

In folktales, events often happen in groups of three. Often the hero will get three magic wishes or three chances to complete an impossible task. From what three dangers did Hippolyte rescue Clement and Pauline? (Call on different students. Idea: *A poisoned stream; a poisoned mango; a serpent in their house.*) Are there any other important threes in this story? (Call on different students. Ideas: *The three zombie women; Hippolyte turns to stone in three stages; Clement says he owes Hippolyte his life three times over; the old man passes his hand three times over the statue of Hippolyte to save him.*)

What did Hippolyte do to prevent Pauline from drinking the poisoned water? (Call on a student. Idea: *He ran ahead and muddied the water.*) How did he stop his friends from eating the poisoned mango? (Call on a student. Idea: *He said they were poison and showed them his blistered hands after touching one.*) How did he save his friends from the snake? (Call on a student. Idea: *He cut the serpent in half with a cutlass.*)

Why did Pauline and Clement suspect Hippolyte wanted to harm them? (Call on different students. Ideas: *Monsieur Zabocat lied; the serpent vanished after it was killed; Hippolyte refused to explain his actions.*) What did Monsieur Zabocat say to persuade Clement that his friend wished him harm? (Call on different students. Idea: *He said Hippolyte was jealous of his friends' happiness, that the sword was proof, and that Hippolyte was a liar and an assassin.*)

Let's discuss the resolution of the story. Raise your hand if you can remember the good deed that Hippolyte and Clement performed near the beginning of the story. (Call on a student. Idea: *They stopped to give a dead beggar a proper burial.*) How did this good deed help the two young men at the end of the story? (Call on a student. Idea: *The old man who saved Hippolyte was the beggar to whom they gave a Christian burial, and the beggar was given permission to come back to Earth to express his gratitude by doing the boys a service in return.*)

Theme

What do you think is the theme of *The Faithful Friend*? (Call on different students. Idea: *The value of true friendship is such that a friend may sacrifice his life to save yours.*) What other values or morals do you think this story teaches? (Call on different students. Idea: *Kindness towards strangers is often repaid.*)

Language

From what you have read in the story, what do you think the greeting *bonjou', Missie* (Pronounced: BOH-zhew) means? (Call on a student. Idea: *Hello, Mistress.*) What do you think what *bonjou', Monfi* means? (Call on a student. Idea: *Hello, my son.*) What parts of the story give you clues about what these greetings mean? (Call on different students. Ideas: *Missie is a word used in English; Monsieur Zabocat and Clement politely exchange greetings when they first meet.*)

When the Hippolyte says that Monsieur Zabocat is a *quimboiseur* (Pronounced: kwim-BWAH-sur), how can you guess what *quimboiseur* means? (Call on a student. Idea: *It is rumored that Zabocat is a wizard.*)

You are told that a *fer de lance* (Pronounced: fair deh LON-seh) is the deadliest snake on Martinique. How do you know what it looks like? (Turn to the appropriate page if students need prompting. Call on a student. Ideas: *It is described as a long, dark, speckled ribbon that glides out from under the bed; it is shown in the illustration.*)

The beggar to whom the young men gave a Christian burial says that *Bon-Die* (Pronounced: Bohn-DEHW) gave him permission to come down to Earth after he died. From this explanation, can you guess who *Bon-Die* is? (Call on a student. Ideas: *The good Lord; God.*)

Summarizing the Literary Analysis

Let's remember some of the things we learned about *The Faithful Friend,* and I'll write them down for you.

What is the purpose of this folktale? (Call on a student. Idea: *To teach a lesson.* Record on chart.)

Is there a moral or value taught in this story? (Call on a student. Ideas: *Kindness is often rewarded with gratitude; the value and faithfulness of a good friend; courage and love can lead to great sacrifices.* Record on chart.)

Who are the main characters in this story? (Call on different students. Ideas: *Clement, Hippolyte, Pauline, Monsieur Zabocat.*) What are some character traits of each of these characters? (Call on different students. Ideas: *Clement and Hippolyte are high-spirited; Hippolyte is cautious and loyal; Pauline is cheerful and spirited; Monsieur Zabocat is evil, furious.*)

What is the theme of the story? (Call on a student. Idea: *The value of true friendship is such that a friend may sacrifice his life to save yours.* Record on chart.)

Independent Reading Selection:

   Dove Isabeau by Jane Yolen.

ADDITIONAL LITERATURE

Following are some additional titles that your students may enjoy during and following this lesson.

   Faithful John or Faithful Joannes by the Brothers Grimm

Activity

Writing/Speaking

Title: Language Log
   Time Required: 15 minutes
   Materials Required: Student notebooks

Procedure

1. (Write the following words on the chalkboard or an overhead transparency: **shachi, shogun, bubog tree, ganta-measure, centavos, quimboiseur, Bon-Die, Missie, Monfi, bonjou', fer de lance.**)

2. English is a language that uses many borrowed and adopted words from different cultures. In the books you have heard and read so far, you have learned many new words. Let's review a few of them. (Point to the words on the chalkboard.) Read these words aloud. (Signal.) (Read words with students.) Raise your hand if you can remember what a *shachi* is. (Call on a student. *Dolphin.*) (Review the remainder of the words.)

3. Sometimes words from other cultures have been used in the English language for such a long time that everybody knows what they mean. (Write **bamboo** on the chalkboard.) What word? (Signal.) *Bamboo.* The word **bamboo** was originally a Malaysian word, but it has been adopted into English. Raise your hand if you can tell us what **bamboo** is. (Call on a student. Idea: *A slim, long, flexible tree that grows in sections and has long, slim leaves.*)

4. The word **lime** came from the Arabic language a long time ago. Raise your hand if you can predict what country the word **banana** was originally from. Remember, bananas grow in warm countries, so you know the word didn't come from Greenland. (Call on different students. Accept two or three responses.) **Banana** is a Portuguese or Spanish word. Raise your hand if you can predict what language **papaya** is from. (Call on different students. Accept two or three responses.) **Papaya** is a Spanish word. Raise your hand if you can predict where the word **zombie** originated. (Call on different students. Accept two or three responses.) **Zombie** came into English from Haiti and West Africa.

5. In your notebooks, begin a language log of all the words you learn that came from another culture. Often, words that describe things that don't normally grow or exist in North America come from other cultures where these things are commonly found.

6. Start a new page in your notebook. Write words that come from another culture next to the margin of your page. Beside them, write their definitions. Finally, write the original nationality after the definition in parentheses. Add to your language log as you come across new words in your reading. You may wish to illustrate each word to help you remember the meaning.

Read each sentence carefully. Decide which of the homonyms in brackets is correct. Then write the correct homonym on the line provided. You may use a dictionary to help you decide which spelling is correct.

1. Mrs. Palomino bought a pound of _____ (meat, meet) at the supermarket.

2. After the wildfire, the hillside was left _____ (bare, bear).

3. It's _____ (plain, plane) that this _____ (plain, plane) will be late.

4. (There, Their, They're) _____ going to be upset when they see that

    (there, their, they're) car is parked over _____ (there, their, they're).

5. Make sure that you _____ (write, right) down the _____ (write, right) answer.

6. Scott _____ (rode, road) his bike down the _____ (rode, road) to Sam's house.

7. Please tell Cassandra that _____ (there, their, they're) ready for

    _____ (there, their, they're) tests.

8. Only _____ (to, too, two) of you can come _____ (to, too, two) the game with me.

9. Please _____ (board, bored) the _____ (plain, plane) in an orderly fashion.

10. Can we come _____ (to, too, two) the mall with you at _____ (to, too, two) o'clock?

© SRA/McGraw-Hill. Permission is granted to reproduce this page for classroom use.

Lesson 6

Language Skill Development

Listening/Speaking/Writing

Title: Identifying Indefinite Pronouns

Time Required: 20 minutes

Materials Required: A visible corner of chalkboard, an overhead transparency, or a sheet of chart paper to record a class list of indefinite pronouns for students to refer to

Preparation: Write the following sentences on the chalkboard, chart paper or on an overhead transparency, omitting the underlining (the answers):

1. **Help! <u>Somebody</u> do <u>something</u> to save my cat!**
2. **<u>No one</u> was doing <u>anything</u> to help.**
3. **Cats can climb up trees but not <u>all</u> can climb down again.**
4. **<u>Neither</u> of us wanted to climb the tree but <u>each</u> of us felt bad.**
5. **<u>Either</u> you or I must rescue that cat.**
6. **<u>Nothing</u> could be done with <u>everyone</u> in such a panic.**
7. **Can <u>anybody</u> see where the cat is?**
8. **<u>All</u> we could see was <u>something</u> white high up on a branch.**
9. **<u>Someone</u> finally saved the cat.**
10. **<u>One</u> should make sure <u>nothing</u> like this happens to again to <u>anyone</u>.**

When you want to talk about people or things in general and not a specific person or thing, you need to use an **indefinite pronoun.** What do you need to use when you talk about people or things in general and not a specific person or thing? (Signal.) *An indefinite pronoun.*

(Write on the transparency, chart paper, or chalkboard and do not erase: **some, any, many, few, all, one.**) These words are all **indefinite pronouns.** Read the list aloud. (Signal.) *Some, any, many, few, all, one.*

(Write on the chalkboard: **Some of the stars you see are really planets. All of the people clapped their hands.**) Read the first sentence aloud. (Signal.) *Some of the stars you see are really planets.* What is the indefinite pronoun in this sentence? (Touch the class list on the chalkboard.) Look at this list if you need help remembering what words are indefinite pronouns. (Call on a student. *Some.*) Read the second sentence aloud. (Signal.) *All of the people clapped their hands.* What is the indefinite pronoun in this sentence? (Call on a student. *All.*)

(Write on the chalkboard: **Peaches are good but many are mushy. People like to travel but few can afford a trip to Australia.**) Read the first sentence aloud. (Signal.) *Peaches are good but many are mushy.*

What is the indefinite pronoun in this sentence? (Call on a student. *Many.*) Read the second sentence aloud. (Signal.) *People like to travel but few can afford a trip to Australia.* What is the indefinite pronoun in this sentence? (Call on a student. *Few.*)

(Write on the chalkboard: **Make sure that all get on the bus. One does not succeed without trying.**) Read the first sentence aloud. (Signal.) *Make sure that all get on the bus.* What is the indefinite pronoun in this sentence? (Call on a student. *All.*) Read the second sentence aloud. (Signal.) *One does not succeed without trying.* What is the indefinite pronoun in this sentence? (Call on a student. *One.*)

There are three more indefinite pronouns that you need to know. (Add to the class list of indefinite pronouns: **each, either, neither.**) These words are all indefinite pronouns. Read the list aloud. (Signal.) *Each, either, neither.*

(Write on the chalkboard: **My cousins will each graduate in June.**) Read this sentence aloud. (Signal.) *My cousins will each graduate in June.* **Each** means every single one. What's another way of saying **every single one**? (Signal.) *Each.*

(Write on the chalkboard: **You can either have pizza or hot dogs for dinner.**) Read the sentence aloud. (Signal.) *You can either have pizza or hot dogs for dinner.* **Either** means **one or the other.** What's another way of saying **one or the other**? (Signal.) *Either.*

(Write on the chalkboard: **Neither of us is allowed to wear high heels.**) Read the sentence aloud. (Signal.) *Neither of us is allowed to wear high heels.* **Neither** means **not one or the other.** What's another way of saying not **one thing or the other thing**? (Signal.) *Neither.*

(Add to the list of indefinite pronouns begun on chart paper or the chalkboard: **-body, -one, -thing.**) Indefinite pronouns often have endings like **-body, -one,** and **-thing**. **Everybody, someone,** and **anything** are good examples. Raise your hand if you can think of some more indefinite pronouns that have these endings. (Call on different students. Ideas: *Nobody; somebody; no one; everyone; something; nothing.*)

(Point to the sentences that are on the chalkboard.) Copy each sentence. Identify the indefinite pronouns in each sentence by underlining them with your ruler. You may look at the class chart to help you remember which words are indefinite pronouns. There are seventeen indefinite pronouns in these sentences. See if you can find them all.

Literature

In the Beginning: Creation Stories from Around the World

by Virginia Hamilton

"The Pea-Pod Man" (A selection from this collection of creation stories.)

Materials required: A map of the world
Folk Literature Summary Chart started in Lesson 1

> **Note:** After a class discussion of the selected book, an independent reading option of a second book is recommended. The books listed follow similar plot, characterization, and themes. You may wish to have your students read the recommended book independently (or in pairs or groups) and compare and contrast the optional selection by modeling their chart summaries (BLM 1B) on the chart completed during class discussion. At the end of each literature lesson, you will find a cross-cultural list of additional books or stories with similar plots and themes that may be used as supplementary reading for each literature lesson.

Many folktales are told for a purpose. Let's review the four purposes for folk literature. The first purpose for folk literature is: (Signal. Hold up one finger for each purpose.) *To tell about the creation of the world.* The second purpose is: (Signal.) *To explain how things came to be.* The third purpose is: (Signal.) *To entertain.* And the fourth purpose is: (Signal.) *To teach a lesson.* (Repeat until firm.)

Examining the Book

This is the next book that we are going to read and discuss. (Point to the title.) Read the title of the book. (Signal.) *In the Beginning.* Sometimes a book has a subtitle under the main title. What is the subtitle of this book? (Signal.) *Creation Stories from Around the World.* (Point to the author's name on the cover.) Who is the author of this book? (Call on a student. *Virginia Hamilton.* Record on class chart. Point to the illustrator's name on the cover.) Who is the illustrator of *In the Beginning?* (Call on a student. *Barry Moser.*)

Today's book is a collection of stories from around the world. I will read you one of the stories, titled "The Pea-Pod Man," which is an Inuit myth widely known from Siberia to Greenland.

The word **Eskimo** means "raw-flesh eaters." It is more correct to say **Inuit,** which means "the people." What is the word for **the people**? (Signal.) *Inuit.* The Inuit people live in northern Canada and the Far North from Siberia to Greenland. Where do the Inuit people live? (Signal.) *In Canada and the Far North from Siberia to Greenland.*

(Show students the location of Northern Canada, Siberia, and Greenland on a world map.) What is the cultural origin of this story? (Signal.) *Inuit.* (Record on class chart.)

The genre of "The Pea-Pod Man" is a myth. What genre is "The Pea-Pod Man"? (Signal.) *A myth.* (Record on chart.) **Myths** are very old stories about superhuman beings, like gods, heroes, and monsters. These stories sometimes try to explain how things in nature started, such as why the sun rises or why volcanoes erupt. This myth is about Raven, the creator.

Making Predictions

(Show students the front cover illustration as well as the two illustrations within the myth.) Raise your hand if you would like to predict what will happen in the story based on what you see in the illustrations. Tell us what part of the illustration gives you an idea about what is happening. (Call on different students. Accept two or three responses.)

Keeping in mind the title of this piece of folk literature and the fact that it is a myth about Raven and creation, try to predict its purpose. Do you think it will be a creation myth, an explaining story, a trickster tale to entertain, or a story that teaches a lesson? Give a reason to support your prediction. (Call on different students. Accept reasonable responses.)

Reading the Book

Choose one of the two options presented in Lesson 1 for reading the book. If students read parts of the story aloud, remind them of the conventions for being an effective speaker and listener found in Lesson 1.

Occasionally, you may find it beneficial to discuss parts of the story that are complicated or that have unfamiliar vocabulary. Encourage students to check the illustrations, the structure of words, and context to help them decipher unknown words and their meanings.)

Literary Analysis

Let's talk about the setting of this myth. Do you know where this story takes place? (Signal.) *No.* When does this myth happen? (Call on a student. Idea: *When there were no people on Earth.*)

Is there anything in the illustrations or the story itself that tells you about the landscape, people, or culture in the ancient time that this myth takes place? (Call on different students. Ideas: *The dark hair and skin of the characters; the berries and animals listed: raspberries, heathberries, mountain sheep, raven, fish, bear.*)

Who are the main characters in "The Pea-Pod Man"? (Call on different students. Ideas: *Raven; Man.*) What kind of powers does Raven have? (Call on different students. Ideas: *He could turn himself into a man; he could create fruit and animals; he could create people.*) Did Raven expect Man to come out of the pea-pod vine he made? (Signal.) *No.*

How did Raven treat Man? (Call on different students. Ideas: *Raven took care of Man and asked Man if he had anything to eat; Raven brought food for Man and created the animals for him to eat.*) What did Raven create so that Man wouldn't be lonely? (Signal.) *Woman.*

Why do you think that Raven was kind and helpful to Man? (Call on different students. Ideas: *Man was helpless to find food for himself until Raven created food; Raven wanted to help Man because Man was his own creation.*)

Story Problem

What was Man's problem after he came out of the pea-pod? (Call on a student. Idea: *The soft, moving ground made him feel sick.*) What was the cause of Man's problem? (Call on a student. Idea: *The new, soft ground.*) Do you think Man was experienced enough to cope with his situation? (Call on a student. Idea: *No.*) What parts of the story tell you that Man is innocent about his surroundings and not very experienced? (Call on different students. Ideas: *He was just born out of the pea-pod; he didn't know what to do; he didn't even know what water was; he knew that water and food made him feel better, but he didn't understand why.*)

Why do you think that Raven told Man to shut his eyes when he was bringing the animals to life, and to go off a ways so Man couldn't be sure what he was doing? (Call on different students. Ideas: *Raven wanted to keep his magic powers a secret; he didn't want Man to see how he made things in case Man started wanting to create things too.* Accept reasonable responses.)

What worried Raven after he had made the sheep? (Call on a student. Ideas: *Man was delighted with the sheep and looked at all the animals with pleasure; Raven was worried that Man would have nothing to fear and would eat or kill everything.*) The resolution is often the solution to the problem. How did Raven solve his problem? (Call on a student. Idea: *He created a bear.*)

Think about the purpose you predicted for this story before you heard it. Do you want to change your mind about what the purpose of this myth is, or was your prediction accurate? (Call on different students. Accept two or three responses.)

Theme

What do you think the theme of "The Pea-Pod Man" is? (Call on different students. Idea: *To explain how people and animals were created.*) Can you think of another moral or value that you might learn from this myth? (Call on a student. Idea: *Don't be greedy.*) Can you think of ways this creation myth is similar to other creation myths you might know about? (Call on different students. Accept reasonable responses.)

Summarizing the Literary Analysis

Let's remember some of the things we learned about "The Pea-Pod Man," and I'll write them down for you.

What is the purpose of this myth? (Call on a student. Idea: *To explain how people and animals were created.* Record on chart.)

Is there a moral or value taught in this story? (Call on a student. Idea: *Not to be greedy.* Record on chart.)

Who are the main characters in this story? (Call on different students. Idea: *Man; Raven.*)

What is the theme of the story? (Call on a student. Idea: *To explain how people and animals were created.* Record on chart.)

Independent Reading Selections:

In the Beginning is an anthology of creation stories from various cultures.

"Raven and the Pea-pod Man" included in *When the World Was Young* retold by Margaret Mayo.

Lesson 7

Language Skill Development

Usage of Indefinite Pronouns

Time Required: 20 minutes

Preparation: Write the following sentences on the chalkboard or overhead transparency: (Do not copy the words in parentheses; they are the answers.)

1. <u>Dominguez, Chantal, and all the people</u> in the neighborhood went to a barbecue in the park. (*Everybody*)
2. <u>Every single</u> person had a good time. (*Each*)
3. <u>A person</u> left a carton in the fridge with <u>no milk, or juice, or soda</u> in it. (*Somebody/nothing*)
4. <u>Not any person</u> knows who left the empty carton there. (*No one* or *nobody*)
5. <u>A cat, or a bird, or a thing</u> knocked over that vase of flowers. (*Something*)
6. Could <u>a person</u> please tell me what happened? (*someone*)
7. <u>Rudy, Ling, and all the other girls</u> on the team went out for a treat after the game. (*Everyone* or *Everybody*)
8. Can <u>a person</u> give me <u>some job or</u> to do? I'm so bored! (*somebody/anybody*) (*something/anything*)

When you want to talk about people or things in general, and not a specific person or thing, you need to use an indefinite pronoun. What do you need to use when you talk about people or things in general? (Signal.) *An indefinite pronoun.*

(Write on the chalkboard: **some, any, many, few, all, one, each, either, neither.**) These words are all indefinite pronouns. What are **each, either**, and **neither**? (Signal.) *Indefinite pronouns.*

Indefinite pronouns often have endings like **-body, -one,** and **-thing. Everybody, someone,** and **anything** are good examples. Raise your hand if you can think of more indefinite pronouns that have these endings. (Call on different students. Ideas: *Nobody; somebody; no one; everyone; something; nothing.*)

(Write on the chalkboard: **Carlos, Natasha, Lee, and the entire science class knew that a person had let the frogs out.**) Read this sentence aloud. (Signal.) *Carlos, Natasha, Lee, and the entire science class knew that a person had let the frogs out.* (Underline **Carlos, Natasha, Lee, and the entire science class.**) Raise your hand if you can think of an indefinite pronoun to replace Carlos, Natasha, Lee, and the entire science class in this sentence. (Call on a student. Ideas: *Everybody, everyone.* Write student's response above the underlined subject.) Let's read this sentence again, replacing that list of people with **everyone** (or **everybody**). (Signal.) *Everyone knew that a person had let the frogs out.* Does the sentence still make sense? (Signal.) *Yes.*

We can make this sentence even shorter by substituting an indefinite pronoun for the words **a person.** (Underline a person.) Raise your hand if you can think of an indefinite pronoun to replace **a person.** (Call on a student. Idea: *Someone.* Write **someone** above **a person.**) Let's read this sentence again, replacing **a person** with **someone.** (Signal.) *Everyone knew that someone had let the frogs out.* Does the sentence still make sense? (Signal.) *Yes.*

(Point to the sentences on the chalkboard. Rewrite each sentence replacing the underlined parts of the sentence with an indefinite pronoun.)

Literature

The Great Race

by David Bouchard

Materials required: A map of the world
Folk Literature Summary Chart started in Lesson 1

> **Note:** After a class discussion of the selected book, an independent reading option of a second book is recommended. The books listed follow similar plot, characterization, and themes. You may wish to have your students read the recommended book independently (or in pairs or groups) and compare and contrast the optional selection by modeling their chart summaries (BLM 1B) on the chart completed during class discussion. At the end of each literature lesson, you will find a cross-cultural list of additional books or stories with similar plots and themes that may be ued as supplementary reading for each literature lesson.

Examining the Book

This is the next book that we are going to read and discuss. (Point to the title.) Read the title of the book. (Signal.) *The Great Race.* (Point to the author's name on the cover.) Who is the author of this book? (Call on a student.) *David Bouchard.* (Record on class chart. Point to the illustrator's name on the cover.) Who is the illustrator of *The Great Race*? (Call on a student. *Zhong-Yang Huang.*)

Today's book is a legend from China. (Show students the location of China on a world map.) Where is the origin of this story? (Signal.) *China.* (Record on class chart.)

The genre of *The Great Race* is a fable. What genre is *The Great Race*? (Signal.) *A fable.* (Record on chart.) A fable is a short story with animal characters that teaches a lesson about human nature. What is a fable? (Signal.) *A short story with animal characters that teaches a lesson about human nature.*

The genre of *The Great Race* is also a **pourquoi** (Pronounced: poor-kwah) **tale.** What genre is *The Great Race*? (Signal.) *A pourquoi tale.* **Pourquoi** is a French word that means **why.** What does **pourquoi** mean? (Signal.) *Why.* A **pourquoi tale** explains why animals have the characteristics that they do. For example, a **pourquoi tale** might tell about why spiders weave webs or why roosters are proud.

Making Predictions

(Open up the front and back covers of the book so that students see the picture in its entirety.) Raise your hand if you would like to predict what will happen in the story based on what you see in the illustrations. Tell us what part of the illustration gives you an idea about what is happening. (Call on different students. Accept two or three responses.)

Keeping in mind the title of this folktale and the fact that it is a fable and a pourquoi tale about the Chinese zodiac, try to predict its purpose. Do you think it will be a creation myth, an explaining story, a trickster tale to entertain, or a story that teaches a lesson? Give a reason to support your prediction. (Call on different students. Accept reasonable responses.)

Reading the Book

Choose one of the two options presented in Lesson 1 for reading the book. If students read parts of the story aloud, remind them of the conventions for being an effective speaker and listener found in Lesson 1.

Occasionally you may find it beneficial to discuss parts of the story that are complicated or that have unfamiliar vocabulary. Encourage students to check the illustrations, the structures of words, and context to help them decipher unknown words and their meanings.)

Literary Analysis

Sometimes, books tell a story within a story. Who are the first two characters you meet in *The Great Race*? (Call on a student. Idea: *A grandmother and a girl.*) What problem does the girl have? (Call on a student. Idea: *She has forgotten the order of the animals in the zodiac.*) How does the grandmother solve the girl's problem? (Call on a student. Ideas: *By telling her a story that explains how the order of the animals came to be; by helping her learn and remember the correct order of the animals in the zodiac.*)

Let's talk about the setting of this first part of the story. Where does this part of the story take place? (Call on a student. Ideas: *In a room; by the girl's bed.*) When does this part of the story happen? (Call on a student. Idea: *Tonight.*)

Now let's talk about the setting of the main part of the story. Where does the main part of the story take place? (Call on a student. Idea: *Across the sea from the Jade City.*)

When does the main story happen? (Call on a student. Ideas: *Long ago, when the moon was young.*)

Most stories are told in **chronological order. Chronological order** means that events are told in the exact time order in which they originally happened. What does chronological order mean? (Signal.) *Events are told in the exact time order in which they originally happened.*

The first part of the story takes place tonight, so it is set in the present time. Then, suddenly, David Bouchard interrupts his story of the grandmother and the little girl to tell another story that happened long ago before the grandmother was born. When a story is interrupted to tell about another event that happened in the past, it is called a **flashback.** What is it called when the story is interrupted to tell about another event that happened in the past? (Signal.) *A flashback.*

At the end of the book, David Bouchard suddenly moves back into the present and continues the story of the grandmother and the girl. Which part of *The Great Race* is a flashback? (Call on a student. Idea: *The story of the animals racing to the Jade City.*) Which part is told in the present time? (Call on a student. Idea: *The story of the grandmother and the girl.*)

Is there anything in the illustrations or the story itself that tells you about the landscape or culture of China in the ancient time in which this folktale takes place? (Call on different students. Ideas: *The names of Great Buddha and Jade City; rocky hill; desert; forest; a mountain range covered with snow; a vast sea.*) How does the setting affect the plot of the story? (Call on different students. Idea: *The story finishes when all the animals have crossed the desert, the forest, the mountains, and finally the sea to reach the Jade City.*)

Who are the main characters in *The Great Race*? (Call on different students. Ideas: *Pig; dog; rooster; dragon; ox; snake; horse; rabbit; goat; monkey; tiger; rat.*) Each of the animals has a particular characteristic. Raise your hand if you can remember the pig's characteristic. (Call on a student. Idea: *He's reliable.* Repeat for the remainder of the animals.)

Which animals were friends in this fable? (Call on a student. Idea: *Pig and dog.*) What does the dog do in the story that demonstrates his loyalty? (Call on a student. Idea: *He stays behind to help his friend.*) How do the dog and the pig help each other? (Call on different students. Ideas: *The dog knows the pig will die if he stays by himself; the pig knows how to find food and water under the ground.*) What values are important to the dog? (Call on different students. Ideas: *Loyalty; friendship; kindness; helpfulness.*) What values are important to the pig? (Call on different students. Ideas: *Fairness; friendship; helpfulness.*)

Many of these animals, like the pig, the goat, the rabbit, and the lion, recognize and accept their weaknesses. The pig knows that he is slow and is resigned to being last in the race. The dog accepts that his friend is slow and stays friends with him anyway. What qualities do the goat, the rabbit, and the tiger recognize and accept in themselves? (Call on a student. Ideas: *The goat knows that he is timid, and that the attention of the race would make him uncomfortable; the rabbit knows that neither he nor the tiger likes water, so they decide to alter their plans.*)

Do you think that the theme of self-acceptance is still an issue today? How? (Call on different students. Accept two or three responses.)

(Turn to the page before the illustration of the rooster attacking the fox. Reread the passage where the rooster addresses the chickens and they reply.) **Formal language** is when you use words politely and with respect. **Informal language** is when you use slang or casual words with your friends. When the rooster addresses the chickens, does he use formal or informal language? (Signal.) *Formal language.* Does the chicken reply using formal or informal language? (Signal.) *Formal.*

How do the rooster and the chicken act and behave together? (Call on different students. Ideas: *The chicken simpers and fluffs her feathers; she flatters the rooster by calling him courageous and hints that a husband would have to be extremely brave to live with them; the rooster puffed himself up, crowed, and beat his wings.*) What is the purpose of their polite language and flirtatious behavior? (Call on a student. Idea: *The rooster wants to convince the chicken that he should live with them, and the chicken is trying to entice the rooster to stay.*)

Why does the monkey drop out of the race? (Call on a student. Idea: *He would rather look at his handsome reflection in the pool all day.*) What reasons does the goat give for giving up on the race? (Call on a student. Ideas: *He's timid; he realizes that this spot contains all the things he needs in life.*)

Why did the snake want to become friends with the horse? (Call on a student. Idea: *Because he wanted the horse to carry him.*) What did he promise the horse he would help him with? (Call on a student. Idea: *Seeing in the dark forest.*) What quality in the horse led to the snake and him becoming lost in the forest? (Call on a student. Idea: *Stubborness.*)

The rabbit tries to strike a deal with the tiger. What is the deal? (Call on a student. Idea: *That they will negotiate the order of arrival in the city and work together to find a safer way to the Jade City than across the ocean.*) Does the rabbit manage to persuade the tiger? (Signal.) *No.*

What cruel trick does the rat play on the ox when the rat spots land? (Call on a student. Idea: *He lies and tells the ox that they will never reach land, then swims to shore by himself when the ox turns back.*) How does the ox feel when he notices the rat is missing from his back? (Call on a student. Ideas: *He is full of grief and guilt; he thinks he has been careless; he's very upset.*)

How does the grandmother say the race turned out? (Call on different students. Ideas: *The tiger and the rabbit came the long way around and finished third and fourth; the dragon came in fifth after chasing away the eight wolves; the ox came in second.*) Does the grandmother ever tell what animal came in first? (Signal.) *No.* How do you know that the cunning rat came in first? (Call on a student. Ideas: *The rat is the only animal not yet placed; first place is the only position left.*)

Some Chinese people believe that each person's personality is influenced by the animal associated with the year in which they were born. By paying close attention to the grandmother's actions and the way she words her story, can you guess under which animal of the zodiac she was born? Justify your response with examples from the story. (Call on different students. Ideas: *She was probably born in the year of the ox because at the beginning of the story she stops listing the animals at the ox and lets her fingers linger on the cutout of the ox; she stops telling details of the story just when the ox heads for the Jade City gates; she gently picks up the cutout of the ox again at the end of the story, and her words emphasize the ox's good heart.)*

Think about the purpose you predicted for this folktale before you heard it. Do you want to change your mind about what the purpose of this fable is, or was your prediction accurate? (Call on different students. Accept two or three responses.)

Theme

What do you think is the theme of *The Great Race*? (Call on different students. Idea: *There are more important things than being the fastest or the most cunning.*) Can you think of another moral or value that you might learn from this myth? (Call on a student. Idea: *Not to be too greedy.*)

Point of View

There are three narrative points of view that an author can use to write a story. These points of view are called **first person, second person,** and **third person.** What are the three points of view that an author can use to write a story? (Signal.) *First person, second person, and third person.*

The most common point of view that an author uses to tell a story is **third person.** What is the most common point of view that an author uses to tell a story? (Signal.) *Third person.* Third person narrative refers to the main characters using the words **he, she,** or **they,** or uses the characters' first names.

(Write on the chalkboard: **Virginia ran out of the park. "There's something in there," she gasped.**) Read the two sentences aloud. (Signal.) *Virginia ran out of the park. "There's something in there," she gasped.* Does the author use the words **he, she,** or the **character's first name**? (Signal.) *Yes.* In what point of view is this narrative written? (Signal.) *Third person.*

Another common point of view that an author uses to tell a story is **first person.** First person narrative is written from the point of view of the main character. You can easily recognize first person narrative because the author uses the words **I** and **me.** What words help you easily recognize first person narrative? (Signal.) *I and me.*

(Write on the chalkboard: **I was running, when suddenly I heard a noise behind me.**) Read the sentence aloud. (Signal.) *I was running, when suddenly I heard a noise behind me.* Does the author use the word **I** or **me** in this example? (Signal.) *Yes.* In what point of view is this narrative written? (Signal.) *First person.*

The least common point of view is **second person.** Second person narrative is written so that the author is directly addressing the reader. You can easily recognize second person narrative because the author uses the words **you** and **your.** What words help you easily recognize second person narrative? (Signal.) *You and your.*

(Write on the chalkboard: **When you need to change your oil, be sure to put a drip pan under your car.**) Read the sentence aloud. (Signal.) *When you need to change* *your oil, be sure to put a drip pan under your car.* Does the author use the words **you** or **your** in this example? (Signal.) *Yes.* In what point of view is this narrative written? (Signal.) *Second person.*

From what point of view is *The Great Race* written? (Call on a student. Idea: *Third person.*)

Summarizing the Literary Analysis

Let's remember some of the things we learned about *The Great Race*, and I'll write them down for you.

What is the purpose of this story? (Call on a student. Idea: *To explain why the animals in the Chinese Zodiac are placed in a certain order.* Record on chart.)

Is there a moral or value taught in this story? (Call on a student. Ideas: *It's not who won that matters; there are things that are more important than being first.* Record on chart.)

Who are the main characters in this story? (Call on different students. Ideas: *Grandmother; the girl; the 12 animals in the zodiak.*)

What is the theme of the story? (Call on a student. Idea: *There are more important things than being the fastest or the most cunning.* Record on chart.)

Independent Reading Selection: "Great Bear" from *Tales of the Shimmering Sky* retold by Susan Milord (Micmac Indian).

When the World Was Young: Creation and Pourquoi Tales retold by Margaret Mayo

ADDITIONAL LITERATURE

Following are some additional titles that your students may enjoy during and following this lesson.

"The Twelve Months" from ***Tales of the Shimmering Sky*** retold by Susan Milord (Slovakian).

"The Division of Day and Night" from ***Tales of the Shimmering Sky*** by Susan Milord (Creek Indian).

Activity

Writing/Speaking

Title: What's Your Sign
   Time Required: 15 minutes
   Materials Required: One copy of the book *The Great Race*

Procedure

1. (Read students the author's note on the Chinese Zodiac at the back of the book.) In what point of view is this part of *The Great Race* written? (Call on a student. Idea: *Second person.*) How do you know that this part of the story is written in second person narrative? (Call on a student. Idea: *Because the author is addressing the reader directly using the word **you.***)

2. (Read aloud the characteristics of the signs for the years in which the students were born or have students independently read the information on the twelve signs of the zodiac.)

3. (Summarize the characteristics for the animal on a cluster that is drawn on the chalkboard.)

4. Write a paragraph that compares your personality to the characteristics of the animal for the year you were born.

5. Choose one characteristic that is true or not true about yourself. Write a second paragraph that is a short anecdote that explains why this characteristic is or is not true for your personality. When we write an anecdote, we write a short story about an event that shows why this characteristic is true or not. For example, I might tell about a time that I kept getting bucked off my horse, but kept getting back on, to support the fact that I am a stubborn person.

6. (Ask students to read their paragraphs aloud to a partner, to a small group, or to the class.)

Activity

Writing

> ### Title: Modern-Day Legend
> **Time Required:** 60 minutes
>
> **Materials Required:** A variety of folk literature that explains why something exists today

Procedure

1. (Ensure that students have read a variety of folktales that explain why something exists today.) Now that you have read several tales that explain why things exist, you will write a modern-day legend of your own. Think about a special place, an unusual plant or animal, or a real event that happened in the past and was important to your community. You might consider land formations near where we live like mountains or unusual rocks, a strange-looking tree in the park, an unusual plant or flower that grows in this area, an animal that lives only in this state, a nearby lake or waterfall, or an unusual or famous building.

2. Using your imagination, come up with a creative reason to explain how and why this natural formation, plant, animal, or building exists today. Think about how or why it might have been created. What kinds of characters might be involved in its history?

3. First make a plan that is an outline of your story. Be sure to include setting, characters, and the story plot on your plan. Your plan may be an outline, a diagram of your story, or a story map.

4. Now think about how you want to tell this story. Would you like your legend to tell a story in chronological order, or do you want to use a flashback? Legends are told using third person narrative, so be sure to use third person point of view when you write your legend by using the names of your characters, and the words **he, she,** or **they** when you refer to your characters.

5. Next, using the information you wrote down on the webchart, draw an outline that tells the basic plot, setting, and characters in your legend.

6. When your plan is organized, write the first draft of your legend. Ask yourself: Have I included all the information the reader needs to know? Have I included any extra details that distract the reader from my main story line? Are my characters realistic and believable? Ask a friend or relative to read your draft and help you decide what ideas need to be changed or developed further.

7. (Encourage students to use a computer or wordprocessor to write the final copies of their literary reviews. Ensure that students follow the correct formatting conventions for margins, tabs, spacing, columns, and paging.)

8. Read your legend aloud to a friend, the class, or a parent or relative. Remember to use appropriate rate, volume, and tone and to speak clearly and project your voice. Make eye contact with your audience, and use gestures and expression to make your speaking more interesting.

Technology:

There are many Internet sites and software writing programs with examples of mind mapping. You may wish to have students access this information to assist them with developing a plan for their stories. Students may word process stories and illustrate them using various graphics programs. Some students may enjoy using animation programs to make their stories come alive on screen. Students may also find many sites on the Internet that provide them with bibliographies of multicultural folk literature. Electronic encyclopedia programs offer students information about the various countries where folk literature originated.

Lesson 8

Language Skill Development

Indefinite Pronouns and Compound Subject/Verb Agreement

Time Required: 15 minutes

First let's review what you know about subjects. The **subject** of a sentence tells us who or what that sentence is about. What does the subject tell us? (Signal.) *Who or what a sentence is about.*

Let's think about what you know about **singular** and **plural.** What does **singular** mean? (Signal.) *One person or one thing.* What does **plural** mean? (Signal.) *More than one person or thing.*

Here is a rule about the subject in a sentence. Subjects must agree with their verbs. Tell me the rule about subjects. (Signal.) *Subjects must agree with their verbs.* Singular subjects go with singular verbs. What kind of subjects go with singular verbs? (Signal.) *Singular subjects.* What kind of verbs go with plural subjects? (Signal.) *Plural verbs.*

When two or more subjects are joined by the word **and,** they become a **plural subject**. When do two or more subjects become a plural subject? (Signal.) *When they are joined by the word **and.***

(Write on the chalkboard: **The monkey and the elephant are running away.**) Read the sentence aloud. (Signal.) *The monkey and the elephant are running away.* What is the subject? (Call on a student. *The monkey and the elephant.* Circle the subject.) The two animals are joined with the word **and,** so is the subject singular or plural? (Signal.) *Plural.* The verb **are running** is plural, so it agrees with the plural subject. (Underline **are running** and draw an arrow to **the monkey and the elephant.**) If the subject is plural, then the verb must be plural too.

(Write on the chalkboard: **Lucy and Daniella have their own uniforms.**) Read the sentence aloud. (Signal.) *Lucy and Daniella have their own uniforms.* What is the subject of this sentence? (Call on a student. *Lucy and Daniella.* Circle **Lucy and Daniella.**) The two girls are joined by the word **and,** so is the subject singular or plural? (Signal.) *Plural.* The verb **have** is plural, so it agrees with **Lucy and Daniella.** (Underline **have** and draw an arrow to **Lucy and Daniella.**)

Here is a rule about indefinite pronouns. Indefinite pronouns ending in **-body, -one** and **-thing** are always singular. When you use an indefinite pronoun like **everybody,** it means that all the people you're talking about are part of one big group. A group is singular, so all the indefinite pronouns that are like groups are singular too.

(Write on the chalkboard: **Everyone on the girls' baseball team has her own uniform.**) Read the sentence aloud. (Signal.) *Everyone on the girls' baseball team has her own uniform.* What's the rule about indefinite pronouns ending with **-body, -one,** or **-thing**? (Call on a student. Idea: *They're always singular.*) **Everyone** has the ending

-one, so it is singular. (Circle **Everyone.**) The verb **has** is singular, so **has** agrees with everyone. (Underline **has** and draw an arrow to **Everyone.**) If the subject is singular, then the verb must be singular too.

Literature

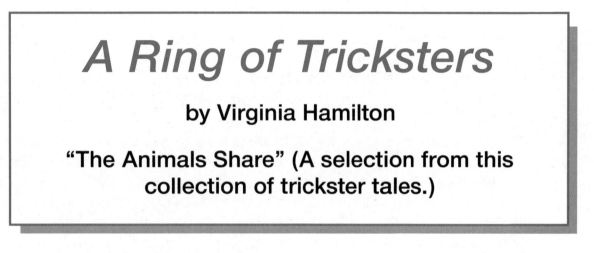

A Ring of Tricksters

by Virginia Hamilton

"The Animals Share" (A selection from this collection of trickster tales.)

Materials required: A map of the world
Folk Literature Summary Chart started in Lesson 1

> **Note:** After a class discussion of the selected book, an independent reading option of a second book is recommended. The books listed follow similar plot, characterization, and themes. You may wish to have your students read the recommended book independently (or in pairs or groups) and compare and contrast the optional selection by modeling their chart summaries (BLM 1B) on the chart completed during class discussion. At the end of each literature lesson, you will find a cross-cultural list of additional books or stories with similar plots and themes that may be used as supplementary reading for each literature lesson.

Examining the Book

This is the next book that we are going to read and discuss. (Point to the title.) Read the title of the book. (Signal.) *A Ring of Tricksters.* Sometimes a book has a subtitle under the main title. What is the subtitle of this book? (Call on a student. *Animals Tales from America, the West Indies, and Africa.* Point to the author's name on the cover.) Who is the author of this book? (Call on a student. *Virginia Hamilton.* Record on class chart. Point to the illustrator's name on the cover.) Who is the illustrator of *A Ring of Tricksters*? (Call on a student. *Barry Moser.*)

Today's book is a collection of trickster tales from America, the West Indies, and Africa. (Show students the location of America, the West Indies, and Africa on a world map.) I will read one of the African stories, which is titled "The Animals Share." What is the title of the African story that you will hear? (Signal.) *"The Animals Share."* Where is the origin of this story? (Signal.) *Africa.* (Record on class chart.)

The genre of "The Animals Share" is a trickster tale. What genre is "The Animals Share"? (Signal.) *A trickster tale.* (Record on chart.) A trickster tale is a short, entertaining story about a clever, tricky animal that outwits others to get what it wants. What is a trickster tale? (Signal.) *A short, entertaining story about a clever, tricky animal that outwits others to get what it wants.*

Making Predictions

(Show students the front cover, as well as a few of the illustrations from "The Animals Share.") Raise your hand if you would like to predict what will happen in the story based on what you see in the illustrations. Tell us what part of the illustration gives you an idea about what is happening. (Call on different students. Accept two or three responses.)

You already know that a trickster tale is about a clever, tricky animal that outwits others to get what it wants. You also know that this tale is from Africa, and that the title is "The Animals Share." Based on all this information, raise your hand if you can make a prediction about what will happen in this story. Tell about a trick that might happen, what trouble you think the main character will get into, and how he gets out of trouble. (Call on different students. Accept two or three responses.)

Reading the Book

Choose one of the two options presented in Lesson 1 for reading the book. If students read parts of the story aloud, remind them of the conventions for being an effective speaker and listener found in Lesson 1.

Occasionally you may find it beneficial to discuss parts of the story that are complicated or that have unfamiliar vocabulary. Encourage students to check the illustrations, the structures of words, and context to help them decipher unknown words and their meanings.)

Literary Analysis

Let's talk about the setting of this story. Where does the story take place? (Call on a student. Idea: *Africa.*) When does the story happen? (Call on a student. Idea: *Long ago.*)

Is there anything in the illustrations or the story itself that tells you about the landscape, different kinds of animals, or culture of Africa? (Call on different students. Ideas: *Not very much rain; dry plains and hills; elephants; lions; tortoises; zebras; hares; bush-buck; buffalo; hyena; the unique names of the characters.*) How does the setting affect the plot of the story? (Call on a student. Idea: *The lakes are dry and there has been no rain, so the animals need to dig a well to find water.*)

Who are the main characters in "The Animals Share"? (Call on different students. Ideas: *King Lion; Shulo the hare; Hamba the tortoise.*) What kind of animal is King Lion? (Call on different students. Ideas: *Merciful; powerful; full of authority*). What kind of animal is Hamba the tortoise? (Call on different students. Ideas: *Old; very wise; clever; patient.*) What kind of animal is Shulo the hare? (Call on different students. Ideas: *Lazy; clever; tricky; sly.*)

Story Problem

What was the animals' problem at the beginning of the story? (Call on a student. Ideas: *The lakes were dried up; there had been no rain.*) What was the cause of their problem? (Call on a student. Idea: *A drought.*)

How does King Lion decide to solve their problem? (Call on a student. Idea: *He instructed the animals to dig a well.*) Which animal doesn't do his part to help? (Signal.) *Shulo the hare.* The animals thought that by dancing, they could kick up the ground and dig that way. What happened instead? (Call on a student. Idea: *They packed the ground down harder.*) Who found water? (Signal.) *Hamba the tortoise.*

Why does King Lion predict that Shulo the hare will come in the night to steal the water? (Call on different students. Ideas: *He knew that Shulo had done nothing to help; he knew he couldn't trust Shulo.*) What does King Lion's prediction make you think will happen next in the story? (Call on a student. Idea: *Shulo will do something tricky.*) When an author gives the reader a little hint that something might happen later on in the story, it is called **foreshadowing.** What is it called when the author gives the reader a little hint that something might happen later on in the story? (Signal.) *Foreshadowing.*

Was King Lion's prediction accurate? (Signal.) *Yes.* What happened? (Call on a student. Idea: *Shulo tricked Bongo and stole water from the well.*) How does Shulo convince Bongo to get tied up? (Call on a student. Ideas: *He persuades Bongo by tempting him with sweet honey; he tells Bongo that he has something so sweet that whoever has a second taste must be tied up.*) Does Shulo's persuasion convince Bongo? (Signal.) *Yes.* Did Shulo fulfill his promise and give Bongo a second taste after he was tied up? (Signal.) *No.*

After Shulo filled his water gourds from the well, why do you think he jumped into the water and splashed around to make it dirty? (Call on different students. Ideas: *Shulo didn't want anyone else to drink the water; he was mean and greedy; he wanted the water all for himself.*) Do you think that Shulo demonstrated good values compared to the other animals? Explain why or why not. (Call on different students. Ideas: *Shulo did not share the water or help to dig it. He stole and lied and made life difficult for the other animals.*) Think of a time in your life when you were not helpful, or when a person you know wasn't helpful, or made life difficult for others. Later on you will use this event in a writing activity.

Who finally outwitted Shulo and how did he do it? (Call on a student. Ideas: *Hamba the tortoise, hid at the bottom of the well and caught Shulo by the foot.*)

What did King Lion say to Shulo? (Call on different students. Ideas: *You wouldn't help dig the well; you stole the water; you made the well all muddy; you must not live another day.*) Which part of what King Lion said was fact, and which part was opinion? (Call on a student. Ideas: *All the things that Shulo did were facts; the judgment that Shulo shouldn't live another day is King Lion's opinion.*)

How did Shulo manage to escape? (Call on different students. Ideas: *He begged permission to sing one song and dance one dance. The animals danced and clapped to the delightful music, and kicked up a thick cloud of dust. Shulo escaped without being seen.*) Knowing how clever and tricky Shulo was, would you have granted his wish? (Call on different students. Accept two or three responses.)

Do you think that granting the wish was a merciful or foolish thing to do? (Call on different students. Accept one or two responses.)

Theme

What do you think is the theme of "The Animals Share"? (Call on different students. Idea: *Those who do not do their share of work shouldn't have a share in the benefits*.) Can you think of another moral or value that you might learn from this myth? (Call on a student. Idea: *That if everyone cooperates and works hard, they can achieve a difficult goal*.)

Onomatopoeia

(Read aloud the first rhyme that the animals dance to.) The animals are doing a joggy-jog trot as they dance. What do you think the line "kuputu kuputu" might mean? (Call on different students. Accept two or three responses.) The words "kuputu kuputu" don't have a meaning. They are spoken in the little song to imitate the sound of animals running.

When a writer uses the way something sounds as a word, it is called **onomatopoeia.** What is it called when a writer uses the way something sounds as a word? (Signal.) *Onomatopoeia.*

(Write on the chalkboard: **hiss, buzz.**) Read the first word. (Signal.) *Hiss.* The way a cat or a snake sounds when it is angry is used as a word, so this is an example of onomatopoeia. Read the second word. (Signal.) *Buzz.* The word **buzz** sounds like what it is describing, so it is an example of onomatopoeia. Raise your hand if you can tell us an example of onomatopoeia. (Call on different students. Ideas: *Moo; mumble; thwack; moan.* Accept correct responses.)

The word **kuputu** is meant to sound like animals running, so is this an example of onomatopoeia? (Signal.) *Yes.*

Summarizing the Literary Analysis

Let's remember some of the things we learned about "The Animals Share," and I'll write them down for you.

What is the purpose of this trickster tale? (Call on a student. Idea: *To entertain and teach a lesson.* Record on chart.)

Is there a moral or value taught in this story? (Call on a student. Ideas: *That we have to accept faults in each other; that even creatures of power like the lion are capable of showing mercy; that those you show mercy to may not be grateful.* Record on chart.)

Who are the main characters in this story? (Call on different students. Ideas: *King Lion; Shulo; Hamba.*)

What is the theme of the story? (Call on a student. Idea: *Those who do not share the work should not share the benefits.* Record on chart.)

Independent Reading Selection: "Cunnie Rabbit and Spider Make a Match" in *A Ring of Tricksters* by Virginia Hamilton (African).

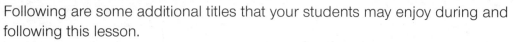

ADDITIONAL LITERATURE

Following are some additional titles that your students may enjoy during and following this lesson.

Any selection from **A Ring of Tricksters** by Virginia Hamilton (American, West Indian, African).

"Catch it and Run!" in **When the World Was Young: Creation and Porquois Tales** by Margaret Mayo (Karok and Klamath Indian).

"The Theft of Thor's Hammer" from **Tales of the Shimmering Sky** by Susan Milord (Scandinavian).

"Sister Fox and Brother Coyote" in **Cut From the Same Cloth: American Women of Myth, Legend, and Tall Tale** by Robert D. San Souci (Mexican American).

"Molly Cottontail" in **Cut From the Same Cloth: American Women of Myth, Legend, and Tall Tale** by Robert D. San Souci (African American).

"The Golden Apples" in **Favorite Norse Myths** retold by Mary Pope Osborne (Norse).

Borreguita and the Coyote: A Tale from Ayutla, Mexico by Verna Aardema

Activity

Writing/Speaking/Listening

Title: Writing a Fable

Time Required: 45 minutes

Materials Required: Lined paper or student notebooks

Procedure

1. In "The Animals Share," all the animals cooperated to dig the well and shared the job of digging. How did the animals react when they found out they would have to work hard? (Call on a student. Ideas: *They grumbled; they were unhappy.*)

2. "All must do their part and take their turn!" roared King Lion when the animals grumbled in the story. Shulo the hare, however, did not work along with all the others. Raise your hand if you can tell us what reason Shulo gave for not helping the others dig the well. (Call on a student. Idea: *He said it would be a waste of his time to dig, and that he would let the others do all the work for him.*) Do you think that this was fair? (Signal.) *No.*

3. Shulo did not share the water or help dig for it. He stole and lied and made life difficult for the other animals. Now, think of a time when you or a person you know wasn't helpful and made life difficult for others, just like Shulo did. You are going to write a fable about this event.

4. When authors write about human values and relationships, they try to make the lesson as fun and entertaining as possible, so that people will want to read the story. Fables use animal characters that act like humans to make the lessons funny and entertaining. Why do fables use animal characters that act like humans? (Signal.) *To make the stories funny and entertaining.* Another reason that authors use animal characters in their stories is so that real people don't have their feelings hurt. Nobody wants to be in a story that shows their bad behavior to everyone else.

5. Now, think of an animal that you could use in your story instead of yourself or the person you were thinking of. Try to pick an animal that could demonstrate the lesson that you think is important with their unique characteristics. Draw a cluster circle on your paper. Write your animal inside the circle. Write the characteristics of your animal on spokes around it.

6. Now you're ready to make a plan or write an outline for your fable. First write down the undesirable behavior of your animal. What motivates your animal to act in the way he or she does? Then decide what setting your animal will be in when it does the undesirable behavior and write down the setting.

7. Next write how this behavior makes the other characters or animals angry or upset. How do they feel? Use descriptive words and comparisons to tell your reader exactly the way everybody feels.

8. What solution do the other characters come up with to solve the problem of your animal's bad behavior? Explain how they work together to teach your main character a lesson. Make someone in your fable use persuasive language to get his or her own way. If you can, use foreshadowing to give your readers a hint about what will happen later in the story. Since you are the author, decide whether you want your point of view to show in the story.

9. Does your animal learn its lesson, or will it continue to cause problems for the other characters or animals? Conclude your fable by writing down the theme or moral of your fable that you want to teach. Can you find another fable that teaches the same lesson that your fable teaches?

10. (Have students use the steps of the writing process outlined in Lesson 7 to write and bring their stories to final copy. Encourage students to write the final copies of their fables on the computer or word processor. Ensure that students follow the correct formatting conventions for margins, tabs, spacing, columns, and paging.)

Lesson 9

Language Skill Development

Identifying Present Perfect Verb Tense

Time Required: 15 minutes

Today you will begin to learn about the perfect verb tense. The perfect verb tense is used when you want to talk about two actions that happened together. Usually, the first action finishes before the second action. There is a present perfect, a past perfect, and a future perfect verb tense. Today you will learn only about the present perfect tense.

(Write on the chalkboard: **Ruby has finished getting dressed, so we can go to the movies.**) Read this sentence aloud. (Signal.) *Ruby has finished getting dressed, so we can go to the movies.*

In this sentence, two actions are happening. What is the first action? (Call on a student. Idea: *Ruby has finished getting dressed*.) Ruby has finished her action right at this exact moment.

What is the second action? (Call on a student. Idea: *We can go to the movies.*) Ruby and her friends can go to the movies right now, because Ruby has just finished getting dressed.

This is the rule that tells you if you need to use the present perfect. If the first action is completed at this exact moment, use the present perfect. When do you use the present perfect verb tense? (Signal.) *When the first action is completed at this exact moment.*

When you use the present perfect, the second action is written in the present. When you use the present perfect verb tense, how is the second action written? (Signal.) *In the present.*

(Write on the chalkboard: **Theo has finished building the house, so we can move in.**) Read this sentence aloud. (Signal.) *Theo has finished building the house, so we can move in.* What is the first action? (Signal.) *Theo has finished building the house.*) Did Theo just finish building the house now? (Signal.) *Yes.* What verb tense is used when the first action is completed at this exact moment? (Signal.) *The present perfect.*

What is the second action? (Call on a student. Idea: *We can move in.*) We can move in right now, because Theo just finished building the house. Is the second action written in the present? (Signal.) *Yes.*

(Write on the chalkboard: **Manda has decided to pay us, so now we can buy groceries.**) Read this sentence aloud. (Signal.) *Manda has decided to pay us, so now we can buy groceries.* What is the first action? (Signal.) *Manda has decided to pay us.* Did Manda just decide to pay us now? (Signal.) *Yes.* What verb tense is used when the first action is completed at this exact moment? (Signal.) *The present perfect.*

What is the second action? (Call on a student. Idea: *We can buy groceries.*) Now we can buy groceries because Manda has just decided to pay us. Is the second action written in the present? (Signal.) *Yes.*

Literature

Medusa

by Deborah Nourse Lattimore

Materials required: A map of the world
Folk Literature Summary Chart started in Lesson 1

Note: After a class discussion of the selected book, an independent reading option of a second book is recommended. The books listed follow similar plot, characterization, and themes. You may wish to have your students read the recommended book independently (or in pairs or groups) and compare and contrast the optional selection by modeling their chart summaries (BLM 1B) on the chart completed during class discussion. At the end of each literature lesson, you will find a cross-cultural list of additional books or stories with similar plots and themes that may be used as supplementary reading for each literature lesson.

Examining the Book

This is the next book that we are going to read and discuss. (Point to the title.) Read the title of the book. (Signal.) *Medusa.* (Point to the author's name on the cover.) Who is the author of this book? (Call on a student. *Deborah Nourse Lattimore.* Record on class chart.) Sometimes the same person who writes the story makes the pictures. Deborah Nourse Lattimore wrote and illustrated this book. Who is the illustrator of *Medusa*? (Call on a student. *Deoborah Nourse Lattimore.*)

Today's book is a Greek myth. (Show students the location of Greece on a world map.) Where is the origin of this story? (Signal.) *Greece.* (Record on class chart.) There are many versions of the Greek myth of *Medusa*, but the version that you will hear today is by Deborah Nourse Lattimore.

The genre of *Medusa* is a myth. What genre is *Medusa*? (Signal.) *A myth.* (Record on chart.) Myths are very old stories about superhuman beings, like gods, heroes, and monsters. These stories sometimes try to explain how things in nature started, such as why the sun rises or why volcanoes erupt. Sometimes myths are hero quests where a hero sets out to achieve a goal. This myth is about a proud girl named Medusa and a hero named Perseus.

Making Predictions

(Open up the front and back covers of the book so that students see the picture in its entirety.) Raise your hand if you would like to predict what will happen in the story based on what you see illustrated on the cover. Tell us what part of the illustration gives you an idea about what is happening. (Call on different students. Accept two or three responses.)

You already know that a myth is about supernatural beings that sometimes explains how things came to be. You also know that this tale is from Greece, and that it is about a proud girl named Medusa and a hero named Perseus. Based on all this information, raise your hand if you can make a prediction about what will happen in this story. Tell about how Medusa's pride might get her into trouble, and predict how she will get out of trouble. What heroic deed do you predict Perseus might accomplish? (Call on different students. Accept two or three responses.)

Reading the Book

Choose one of the two options presented in Lesson 1 for reading the book. If students read parts of the story aloud, remind them of the conventions for being an effective speaker and listener found in Lesson 1.

Occasionally you may find it beneficial to discuss parts of the story that are complicated or that have unfamiliar vocabulary. Encourage students to check the illustrations, the structures of words, and context to help them decipher unknown words and their meanings.)

Literary Analysis

Let's talk about the setting of this story. Where does the beginning of the story take place? (Call on a student. Idea: *In the muddy depths of the ocean.*) When does the story happen? (Call on a student. Ideas: *In the ancient and mysterious past; when the gods of Greece walked the earth.*)

Is there anything in the illustrations or the story itself that tells you about the landscape, people, or culture of Greece in the ancient time that this myth is told? (Call on different students. Ideas: *Ocean; mountains; islands; cool, white clothes that leave the arms and legs bare; sandals; helmets; swords and shields.*)

Who are the main characters in *Medusa*? (Call on different students. Ideas: *Medusa; Perseus; Athena.*) What kind of person is Medusa at the beginning of the story? (Call on different students. Ideas: *Vain; proud; boastful; beautiful.*) What kind of person is Medusa at the end of the story? (Call on different students. Ideas: *Angry; vengeful; proud; hideous.*) What happens in the story to change Medusa's characteristics? (Call on different students. Idea: *Athena punishes her for her vanity and pride by giving her snakes for hair.*) Which of Medusa's characteristics do not change throughout the story? (Call on a student. Ideas: *Her pride; she is too proud to live with her brother and sisters after being cursed by Athena.*)

What kind of person is Perseus? (Call on different students. Ideas: *Brave; obedient; heroic.*) What kind of person is Athena? (Call on different students. Ideas: *Angry; jealous; helpful; vengeful.*) What kind of person is Polydectes? (Call on different students. Ideas: *Cruel; arrogant; tyrannical.*)

Story Problem

What is Medusa's problem at the beginning of the story? (Call on a student. Idea: *Medusa's hair was changed into snakes and Athena put a curse on her.*) What is the curse? (Call on different students. Idea: *Everyone who looks at Medusa will be turned to stone. One day a boy from the sea will come to kill her.*) Raise your hand if you can remember what it is called when the author tells the reader about something that will happen later on in the story. (Call on a student. *Foreshadowing.*) What future event is foreshadowed? (Call on a student. Idea: *Perseus killing Medusa.*)

What was Perseus and his mother Danae's problem at the beginning of the story? (Call on a student. Idea: *Danae's father shut them in a chest and tossed them out to sea because he was told that Danae's son would one day kill him.*)

What was Perseus and Danae's main problem after they were rescued by the fisherman? (Call on a student. Idea: *An evil king named Polydectes wanted to marry Danae and ordered Perseus to bring back Medusa's head as a wedding gift.*) What was the cause of his problem? (Call on a student. Idea: *Polydectes's desire to marry his mother.*)

Who helps Perseus solve his problem? (Call on a student. Idea: *Athena and Hermes.*) What do Athena and Hermes give Perseus to help him? (Call on a student. Idea: *A shield and a sword.*) What three magic objects help Perseus fight Medusa? (Call on different students. Idea: *Winged golden sandals, a leather pouch, and a Cap of Darkness.*)

In folk literature, events often happen in groups of three. Often the hero will get three magic wishes or three chances to complete an impossible task. The number three is important in this myth as well. Raise your hand if you can think of another part of the story where there are three of something. (Call on different students. Ideas: *The three Gray Sisters; the three nymphs.*)

How did Perseus find a solution to Polydectes's cruelty? (Call on a student. Ideas: *He showed Medusa's head to the evil king when he demanded to see it; he was too arrogant to believe that Perseus really killed Medusa and he taunted the boy.*) Raise your hand if you can tell us which character traits led Medusa to her death. (Call on a student. Idea: *Pride and arrogance.*) Which character traits led Polydectes to his death? (Call on a student. Ideas: *Arrogance; tyranny; greed.*)

The end of this myth explains how red coral came to be. According to the story, what is the explanation for red coral's existence in the oceans? (Call on a student. Idea: *Wherever the blood from Medusa's head trickled into the salty ocean, it turned into bright red coral.*) The myth explains that red coral is the blood of Medusa, so part of its purpose is to explain natural phenomena.

Raise your hand if you can remember any other folk literature that we read where a character turned to stone. (Call on different students. Ideas: *The Faithful Friend; Dove Isabeau.*)

Theme

What do you think the theme of *Medusa* is? (Call on different students. Idea: *Pride and arrogance may be punished.*) Can you think of another moral or value that you might learn from this myth? (Call on a student. Idea: *The courage and persistence of heroes can enable them to achieve their goals. The love a son has for his mother gives him strength to achieve the impossible.*)

Language

(Read the author's note at the beginning of the book aloud.) What does the Greek word **hubris** mean? (Call on a student. Idea: *Arrogance or pride.*) Many people have read the Greek myths that warn about the dangers of **hubris.** The English language has borrowed the Greek word *hubris* to mean arrogance or pride.

Simile

When a writer uses the words **like** or **as** to compare something to something else, it is called a **simile.** What is it called when a writer uses the words **like** or **as** to compare something to something else? (Signal.) *A simile.*

(Write on the chalkboard: **She laughed like a hiccupping hyena. He leaped as clumsily as a three-legged hippo.**) Read the first sentence aloud. (Signal.) *She laughed like a hiccupping hyena.* The word **like** compares the way she laughs to a hiccupping hyena, so this is an example of a simile. Read the second sentence aloud. (Signal.) *He leaped as clumsily as a three-legged hippo.* The word **as** compares how he leaped to a three-legged hippo, so this is an example of a simile. Raise your hand if you can make up your own simile using the words **like** or **as** in a comparing sentence. (Call on different students. Accept correct responses.)

(Turn to the second page of the story and read the fourth sentence aloud.) How does the news travel? (Call on a student. Idea: *As swift as an undersea storm.*) Did you hear the words **like** or **as** used in a comparison? (Signal.) *Yes.* To what does the word **as** compare the way the news travels? (Signal.) *The swiftness of an undersea storm.* So, is this is a simile? (Signal.) *Yes.*

(Turn to the next page and read the second sentence aloud.) Did you hear the words **like** or **as** used in a comparison? (Signal.) *Yes.* To what does the word **like** compare the way Medusa thinks she looks? (Signal.) *A goddess.* So, is this is a simile? (Signal.) *Yes.*

(Turn to the page where Perseus kills Medusa and read the final sentence aloud.) Did you hear the words **like** or **as** used in a comparison? (Signal.) *Yes.* To what is the sword compared? (Signal.) *A silver beam.* The sword is like a silver beam, so is this a simile? (Signal.) *Yes.*

Summarizing the Literary Analysis

Let's remember some of the things we learned about *Medusa*, and I'll write them down for you.

What is the purpose of this myth? (Call on a student. Ideas: *To teach a lesson; to explain how red coral was created.* Record on chart.)

Is there a moral or value taught in this story? (Call on a student. Ideas: *Not to be proud, vain, or arrogant. The power of courage and persistence.* Record on chart.)

Who are the main characters in this story? (Call on different students. Idea: *Medusa, Perseus, Athena, Polydectes.*) What are some character traits of each of these characters? (Call on different students. Ideas: *Medusa is vain, arrogant, proud; Perseus is brave, obedient, heroic; Athena is angry, powerful, helpful; Polydectes is arrogant, tyrannical, cruel, unfair.*)

What is the theme of the story? (Call on a student. Idea: *Bragging and arrogance may be punished.* Record on chart.)

Independent Reading Selection: *Perseus* retold by Warwick Hutton.

ADDITIONAL LITERATURE

Following are some additional titles that your students may enjoy during and following this lesson.

Selections of myths that tell of heroes defeating monsters.

"Perseus and the Gorgon's Head" in **Greek Myths** retold by Jacqueline Morley.

"Pegasus: The Chimera" in **Mythical Birds & Beasts From Many Lands** by Margaret Mayo.

Pegasus, the Flying Horse by Jane Yolen.

Pegasus by Marianna Mayer.

"The Magic Stallion" in **Favorite Norse Myths** retold by Mary Pope Osborne.

"Yakami" in **Women Warriors** by Marianna Mayer (Chinese). Note: This book contains a wonderful world map of women warriors from around the world.

"Devi" in **Women Warriors** by Marianna Mayer (East Indian).

"Hekeke" in **Cut From the Same Cloth: American Women of Myth, Legend, and Tall Tale** by Robert D. San Souci (Miwok).

Hercules by Robert Burleigh.

"The Twelve Labours of Heracles" in **Greek Myths** retold by Jacqueline Morley.

Additional Selections with pride and arrogance as a central theme:

"The Story of Arachne" in **Greek Myths** retold by Jacqueline Morley.

"The Boastful Star" in **Tales of the Shimmering Sky** retold by Susan Milord (Polynesian).

Activity

Writing/Reading/Speaking

Title: Writing a Literary Review

Time Required: 60 minutes

Materials Required: Student notebooks

Preparation: Draw the following blank chart on the chalkboard:

Medusa		Title of second myth	
Strengths		Strengths	
Weaknesses		Weaknesses	

1. (Ensure that students have read at least two versions of a myth where a hero defeats a monster.) A **literary critic** is a person who reads a book or story and then writes about its strengths and weaknesses. What is a literary critic? (Signal.) *A person who reads a book or story and then writes about its strengths and weaknesses.* Sometimes, a critic compares two or more books or stories and helps others decide which one they would like to read.

2. Today you are all going to be literary critics. You have each heard the story of *Medusa,* and read another myth about a hero who defeated a monster. Turn to a new page in your notebook and copy the chart on the blackboard into your notebook.

3. List what you consider to be the strengths and weaknesses of each book on the chart. You may also wish to comment on the effectiveness of the illustrations. Put a star beside what you think was the most important strength or weakness of each book.

4. Use the information on your chart to help you write a literary review of each book. Clearly explain whether or not the book was effective. How might you have improved the story telling? Were there any parts of the story that were confusing or that could have been more clearly told? Would you have liked more or less detail and/or description?

5. Organize your critical review beginning with what you think was the most important strength or weakness of the book as your first paragraph. Support your statement with examples from the book. Conclude your review by saying whether or not you would recommend the book to someone else, and tell why or why not.

6. (Encourage students to use a computer or word processor to write the final copies of their literary reviews. Ensure that students follow the correct formatting conventions for margins, tabs, spacing, columns, and paging.)

7. (Give students the opportunity to read their literary reviews aloud in groups or to a friend. Ask students if they were persuaded to try reading a myth by listening to the reviews of their classmates.)

Media and technology

Have students find literary reviews of various books using the Internet. Students may also watch reviews on television, listen to them on the radio, or read them in magazines, journals, or newspapers.

Language Skill Development
Identifying Past Perfect Verb Tense
Time Required: 15 minutes

The **perfect verb tense** is used when you want to talk about two actions that happened together. Usually the first action finishes before the second action. Today you will learn about the **past perfect verb tense.**

(Write on the chalkboard: **Mandze had finished cleaning her room, so she went outside.**) Read this sentence aloud. (Signal.) *Mandze had finished cleaning her room, so she went outside.* In this sentence, two actions are happening. What is the first action? (Call on a student. Idea: *Mandze had finished cleaning her room.*) Mandze had finished her action in the past before something else happened.

What was the second action? (Call on a student. Idea: *She went outside.*) Mandze went outside because she had already cleaned her room.

This is the rule that tells you if you need to use the past perfect verb tense. If the first action has already been completed before another action in the past, use the past perfect tense. When do you use the past perfect verb tense? (Signal.) *When the first action has already been completed before another action in the past.*

When you use the past perfect, the second action is written in the past. When you use the past perfect verb tense, how is the second action written? (Signal.) *In the past.*

(Write on the chalkboard: **Anoki had ridden ten miles on his bike, so he stopped for a rest.**) Read this sentence aloud. (Signal.) *Anoki had ridden ten miles on his bike, so he stopped for a rest.* What is the first action? (Call on a student. Idea: *Anoki had ridden ten miles on his bike.*) Anoki had finished his action in the past before something else happened.

What was the second action? (Call on a student. Idea: *He stopped for a rest.*) Anoki stopped for a rest because he had already ridden his bike ten miles. Is the second action written in the past? (Signal.) *Yes.*

(Write on the chalkboard: **Katy had finished washing her car, so she went for a drive.**) Read this sentence aloud. (Signal.) *Katy had finished washing her car, so she went for a drive.* What is the first action? (Call on a student. Idea: *Katy had finished washing her car.*) Katy had finished her action in the past before something else happened.

What was the second action? (Call on a student. Idea: *She went for a drive.*) Katy went for a drive because she had already finished washing her car. Is the second action written in the past? (Signal.) *Yes.*

Literature

The Sea King's Daughter

by Aaron Shepard

Materials required: A map of the world
Folk Literature Summary Chart started in Lesson 1

Note: After a class discussion of the selected book, an independent reading option of a second book is recommended. The books listed follow similar plot, characterization, and themes. You may wish to have your students read the recommended book independently (or in pairs or groups) and compare and contrast the optional selection by modeling their chart summaries (BLM 1B) on the chart completed during class discussion. At the end of each literature lesson, you will find a cross-cultural list of additional books or stories with similar plots and themes that may be used as supplementary reading for each literature lesson.

Examining the Book

This is the next book that we are going to read and discuss. (Point to the title.) Read the title of the book. (Signal.) *The Sea King's Daughter.* (Point to the author's name on the cover.) Who is the author of this book? (Call on a student. *Aaron Shepard.* Record on class chart.) Who is the illustrator of *The Sea King's Daughter*? (Call on a student. *Gennady Spirin.*)

Today's book is a Russian folktale. (Show students the location of Russia on a world map.) Where is the origin of this story? (Signal.) *Russia.* (Record on class chart.) There are many versions of this Russian tale, but the version that you will hear today is by Aaron Shepard.

The genre of *The Sea King's Daughter* is a legend. What genre is *The Sea King's Daughter*? (Signal.) *A legend.* (Record on chart.) A **legend** is a story that has been told by people for a long time. What is a legend? (Signal.) *A story that has been told by people for a long time.* A legend often tells about the marvelous deeds of a hero or a saint. What does a legend often tell about? (Signal.) *The marvelous deeds of a hero or a saint.*

Making Predictions

(Open the front and back covers of the book so that students see the picture in its entirety.) Raise your hand if you would like to predict what will happen in the story based on what you see illustrated on the front cover. Tell us what part of the illustration gives you an idea about what is happening. (Call on different students. Accept two or three responses.)

You already know that a legend is about the marvelous deeds of a hero or a saint, and that this story is set in Russia. Based on this information, raise your hand if you can make a prediction about what will happen in this story. Tell about how the hero might get into trouble, and predict what marvelous deed he or she will perform to get out of trouble. (Call on different students. Accept two or three responses.)

Reading the Book

Choose one of the two options presented in Lesson 1 for reading the book. If students read parts of the story aloud, remind them of the conventions for being an effective speaker and listener found in Lesson 1.

(Occasionally, you may find it beneficial to discuss parts of the story that are complicated or that have unfamiliar vocabulary. Encourage students to check the illustrations, the structures of words, and context to help them decipher unknown words and their meanings.)

Literary Analysis

Let's talk about the setting of this story. Where does the beginning of the story take place? (Call on a student. Idea: *In the river port city Novgorod the Great.*) When does the story happen? (Call on a student. Idea: *Long ago.*)

(Reread page 10 aloud.) Raise your hand if you can tell us what information you learned about the city of Novgorod from the story or from the illustrations. (Call on different students. Ideas: *It is on a river port; it is the richest and most free in all Russia; it has a busy Market Square full of merchants and traders from around the world; there are sailing ships and piers; a Great Bridge over the River Volkhov, white stone churches with gilded roofs.*)

Is there anything in the illustrations or the story itself that tells you about the landscape, people, clothing, or culture of Russia in the ancient time that this legend is told? (Call on different students. Ideas: *Long embroidered dresses; richly decorated long coats; heeled boots; tall, ornamented headdresses and caps; fair skin and blond or brown hair; thick beards; decorated sails on wooden ships; tall spires and domes on buildings; a broad river; the people enjoy music and dancing.*)

Who are the main characters in *The Sea King's Daughter*? (Call on different students. Ideas: *Sadko, the King of the Sea, the Sea Queen, Princess Volkhov.*) What kind of person is Sadko at the beginning of the story? (Call on different students. Ideas: *Lonely, proud of his city, a good man, quick thinking, happy to be a musician*). Does Sadko's character change by the end of the story? (Call on different students. Idea: *No.*)

Story Problem

What is Sadko's problem at the beginning of the story? (Call on a student. Idea: *He is lonely.*) What was the cause of his problem? (Call on a student. Idea: *None of the women he fell in love with would consider marrying him because he was poor.*) Sadko is a good and talented man, but these are not qualities that the women in the story seem to admire. What qualities do you think were important to the women who refused to marry him? (Call on different students. Ideas: *Wealth, money, riches.*) Why did Princess Volkhova love Sadko? (Call on a student. Idea: *He played beautiful music that she loved to listen to.*)

Everybody in the story loves to hear music. Is music important in our society today? (Call on a student. Idea: *Yes.*) Raise your hand if you can tell us a place where you hear and enjoy music every day. (Call on different students. Ideas: *In stores, on the car radio, movie soundtracks, television backgroud music, concerts.*)

What was Sadko's problem when he finished playing his music for the King of the Sea? (Call on a student. Idea: *The King of the Sea wanted him to marry one of his daughters, but if he did Sadko could never return to his beloved city.*) What was the cause of his problem? (Call on a student. Idea: *The Sea King's request that he never return to his beloved city.*)

Who helps Sadko solve his problem? (Call on a student. Idea: *The Queen of the Sea.*) What reason does she give for helping him? (Call on a student. Idea: *He is a good man.*) What does she tell him to do to avoid being trapped under the sea forever? (Call on a student. Ideas: *She tells him the truth, she warns him not to touch Princess Volkhov.*)

How did Sadko find a solution to being trapped under the sea forever? (Call on a student. Idea: *He refused to kiss or touch Princess Volkhov on their wedding night, so he was returned safely to his city.*) Sadko had to make a difficult decision. Raise your hand if you would have made the same choice as Sadko did. (Tally the number of hands.) Raise your hand if you would have stayed under the sea with Princess Volkhova. (Tally the number of hands. Ask various students to give reasons for their point of view.)

The King of the Sea told Sadko that if the world were fair, he would have his fill of riches. At the end of the story, Sadko invests the wealth the King of the Sea gave him and becomes the richest merchant in the city. Do you think the reason he gets married is because he's now a rich man? (Call on different students. Accept one or two responses.) Do you think in today's world, people marry according to the value of love or because of money? (Call on different students. Accept two or three responses.)

Remember, at the beginning of the story, Sadko tells his friends that surviving on so little money is not so bad because he plays the music he loves. How important do you think money really is to Sadko? (Call on different students. Accept two or three responses.) How important is money to you living in today's world? (Call on different students. Accept two or three responses.)

Theme

What do you think the theme of *The Sea King's Daughter* is? (Call on different students. Idea: *The love of home may be stronger than the love of another person.*)

Language

What does the story tell you that a *gusli* (Pronounced: GOOSE-lee) is? (Call on a student. Idea: *A twelve-stringed musical instrument.*) (Show students the first two illustrations of the story.) What does this illustration tell you about how a *gusli* is played? (Call on a student. Idea: *Sitting flat on the knees of the player and plucked with all ten fingers, held with a long strap around the neck.*)

(Read the first two paragraphs of the author's note at the end of the book aloud.) What does the Russian term *byliny* (Pronounced: BIL-lin-ee) mean? (Call on a student. Idea: *What has been.*) What are *byliny*? (Call on a student. Idea: *Epic ballads recited and often accompanied by the gusli.*) What do you think might be some reasons that byliny singing is a dying art in Russia's culture? (Call on different students. Ideas: *People don't have time to hear byliny; people watch television instead of hearing the legends of their culture; not many people remember how to sing byliny.*)

Nuances of Language (Shades of Meaning)

When an author writes a story, he or she chooses words very carefully in order to get the characters' emotions and our visualization of the setting just right. There are many words that have similar meanings but are slightly different.

(Write on the chalkboard: **whisper, mumble.**) Read these words aloud. (Signal.) *Whisper, mumble.* Both these words mean to talk in a soft, low voice, but they don't mean quite the same thing. Raise your hand if you can tell us the difference between **whispering** and **mumbling.** (Call on a student. Idea: *A whisper is soft but the words are clear; a mumble is soft but the words are hard to understand.*)

(Write on the chalkboard: **dripping, trickling.**) Read these words aloud. (Signal.) *Dripping, trickling.* Both these words mean a small amount of running water, but they don't mean quite the same thing. Raise your hand if you can tell us the difference between **dripping** and **trickling.** (Call on a student. Idea: *Dripping means one drop of water falling at a time; trickling means little drops falling continuously.*)

(Turn to page 10 and read the second sentence aloud.) If the author had written that the red sun shone darkly through the water instead of dimly, how would the meaning be different? (Call on a student. Idea: *The image might be frightening instead of mysterious.*) If the author had written that the white stone palace towered in front of Sadko instead of stood in front of him, how would the meaning be different? (Call on a student. Idea: *The palace would make Sadko feel in awe and a little scared instead of welcome.*)

(Read the next sentence aloud.) Instead of passing through the gate, what are some other similar ways that Sadko could walk through? (Call on different students. Ideas: *Stroll, glide, saunter, waltz.* Remind students that the word must have a similar meaning to the original word. **Running** or **flying through** would not be appropriate responses.)

(Read the next sentence aloud.) What two words does the author use to describe the palace and the doors that are similar but not exactly the same? (Call on a student. *Huge and giant.*) Let's switch the order of these two words and say: As he reached the giant palace doors, they swung open to reveal a huge hall. Did the meaning change very much? (Signal.) *No.* Why do you think the author wanted huge palace doors instead of giant ones? (Call on a student. Accept reasonable responses.)

Summarizing the Literary Analysis

Let's remember some of the things we learned about *The Sea King's Daughter,* and I'll write them down for you.

What is the purpose of this folktale? (Call on a student. Ideas: *To teach the importance of music in the lives of people; to teach how important home may be.* Record on chart.)

What morals or values are taught in this story? (Call on a student. Ideas: *Faithfulness to home; the power of love; the power of music.* Record on chart.)

Who are the main characters in this story? (Call on different students. Ideas: *Sadko, the King of the Sea, the Queen of the Sea, Princess Volkhova.*)

What is the theme of the story? (Call on a student. Idea: *The love of home may be stronger than the love of another person.* Record on chart.)

Independent Reading Selection: "The Mermaid" in *Mythical Birds & Beasts From Many Lands* by Margaret Mayo.

ADDITIONAL LITERATURE

Following are some additional titles that your students may enjoy during and following this lesson.

Any version of "The Little Mermaid."

Activity

Reading/Writing

Title: *Shades of Meaning*

Time Required: 20 minutes

Materials Required: Copies of *The Sea King's Daughter* and/or other literature books in class, student notebooks, several thesauruses

Procedure

1. Authors choose the words for their stories very carefully. Changing the word that an author picked to another one that has a similar but not identical meaning can often change the mood or tone of the story. This is because similar words often have different shades of meaning.

2. Using copies of *The Sea King's Daughter* and/or other books that you have read in class, find a sentence in which you would like to try inserting a different word than the one that the author selected. Write the sentence in your notebook.

3. Now think of a word that is very similar to the word you want to change. Rewrite the sentence, substituting the new word for the one the author picked. Make sure that you substitute a word that retains the original idea of the author.

4. (Show students a thesaurus.) A **thesaurus** is a reference book that lists words that have similar meanings. What is a thesaurus? (Signal.) *A reference book that lists words that have similar meanings.* You may use a thesaurus if you have trouble thinking of a word that has a similar meaning.

5. Finally, write how your new word changed the mood or tone of the sentence. Record which version you prefer: the original word the author picked or the new word you chose.

6. Choose a different shade of meaning for at least five different sentences.

Lesson 11

Language Skill Development

Identifying Future Perfect Verb Tense

Time Required: 15 minutes

The **perfect verb tense** is used when you want to talk about two actions that happened together. Usually the first action finishes before the second action. Today you will learn about the future perfect verb tense.

(Write on the chalkboard: **Dominic will have finished learning long division by the time he goes home this afternoon.**) Read this sentence aloud. (Signal.) *Dominic will have finished learning long division by the time he goes home this afternoon.* In this sentence, two actions are happening. What is the first action? (Call on a student. Idea: *Dominic will have finished learning long division.*) Dominic will have finished his action sometime in the future, but before something else happens.

What will be the second action? (Call on a student. Idea: *He will go home in the afternoon.*) Dominic will have learned long division before he does something else in the future.

This is the rule that tells you if you need to use the **future perfect verb tense.** If the first action will be completed before another action in the future, use the future perfect tense. When do you use the future perfect verb tense? (Signal.) *When the first action will be completed before another action in the future.*

(Write on the chalkboard: **Anna will have completed her report before she goes out.**) Read the sentence aloud. (Signal.) *Anna will have completed her report before she goes out.*) What is the first action? (Call on a student. Idea: *Anna will have completed her report.*) Anna will have finished her action sometime in the future, but before something else happens.

What will be the second action? (Call on a student. Idea: *She will go out.*) Anna will have completed her report before doing something else in the future.

Literature

Favorite Norse Myths

retold by Mary Pope Osborne

Examining the Book

Today we are going to read and discuss poetry. First we are going to read a myth about how poetry came to the world. (Point to the title.) Read the title of the book. (Signal.) *Favorite Norse Myths.* (Point to the author's name on the cover.) The myths in this book were retold by Mary Pope Osborne, so she is the author. Who is the author of this book? (Signal.) *Mary Pope Osborne.* Troy Howell created the illustrations for this book. Who illustrated *Favorite Norse Myths*? (Signal.) *Troy Howell.*

What is the genre of the story that I will read to you today? (Signal.) *Myth.* The myths in this book were told by people in Norway thousands of years ago. (Read the introduction to the students or have students take turns reading a portion of the introduction aloud to classmates.)

One of the myths in this book tells about how the Norse god Odin brought poetry to the world.

Reading the Myth

(Show students the illustration.) I'm going to read this myth aloud to you. (Read the myth with minimal interruptions.)

OR

You may also wish to have your students take turns reading parts of the myth aloud to classmates. Remind students of the conventions of being effective speakers and listeners.

Literary Analysis

How does this myth start? (Call on a student. Idea: *With a poem.*)

Plot of the Story

A **quest** is a journey that a character embarks on to achieve a goal. What was the goal of Odin's first quest? (Call on a student. Idea: *Odin wanted to gain all the world's wisdom and memory.*) What did Odin have to do to achieve his goal? (Call on a student. Idea: *Drink from the magic waters of Mimir's Well.*) Sometimes a character has to make sacrifices or has his courage tested when he is on a quest. What sacrifice did Odin have to make to get the water from the well? (Call on a student.) *Odin had to give Mimir one of his eyes.* (Point to the character in the background.) Who is this character? (Signal.) *Mimir.* (Point to Odin.) Who is this character? (Signal.) *Odin.*

What was the goal of Odin's second quest? (Call on a student. Idea: *To learn the secret runes.*) Another way of saying **sacrifice** is to say **the price the person had to pay.** What price did Odin have to pay to get the runes? (Call on a student. Ideas: *Great suffering; hang on a tree for nine days with a sword piercing his side.*) How does this quest relate to the poem that was at the beginning of this myth? (Call on a student. Idea: *It tells about this quest.*)

What was the goal of Odin's third quest? (Call on a student. Idea: *To gain the Mead of Poetry, the drink that turned a person into a poet.*) Explain how Odin got past the trolls. (Call on a student. Idea: *Disguised himself; sharpened the trolls' cutting tools; tricked them by throwing the whetstone into the air.*) How did Odin's trick help him achieve his goal? (Call on a student. Idea: *Baugi needed someone to do his work because the trolls quarreled.*) What did Odin do to finally achieve his goal? (Call on different students. Ideas: *Outwitted Suttung, bore a hole through the mountain; turned into a snake to slither through the hole; stayed with Gunlod and drank the mead; flew away as an eagle; poured the liquid into the jars of the gods.*) What was the result of Odin's third quest? (Call on a student. Idea: *Poetry became the gift of the gods and humans.*)

Learning about Poetry

There are many forms of poetry. We are going to read several kinds of poems and then you will have an opportunity to write and illustrate some poetry of your own.

Poetry is a unique form of writing that allows the writer, called a poet, to use words, phrases, and sentences creatively. There are no specific rules for writing poetry. Poetry enables the poet to be an artist with words. Often poetry creates a mood or strong feelings in the reader or listener. Poetry is often recited, or read aloud, to give the listener a sense of the rhythm of the poem.

Literature

Sing a Song of Popcorn

selected by Beatrice Schenk de Regniers

Reading the Poems

(Assign various students a poem to read aloud to the class from the literature selection. Provide students with a copy of the poem to be read and give them sufficient time to practice reading the poem aloud until they can read it with expression, feeling, and rhythm. You may wish to have students memorize their poems. Encourage students to use the conventions of being a good speaker:)

- Speak clearly and at a volume that can be heard by everyone in your audience.
- You are reading poetry, so you may want to be creative about the words you stress when you speak, how you pace the reading of various parts of your poem, and the pronunciation of words that the poet may have made up.
- Use movements, facial expressions, and gestures to make your poetry reading more meaningful to your audience.
- Poets often pause for short moments of silence when they read or recite a poem. Think about where in your poem this would be an effective strategy.

(Students may enhance their poetry readings by using graphics, illustrations—their own or from other sources, color, motion, overheads, or music.)

Discussing the Poem

(After each student has read his or her selection, have a short discussion to analyze the key components of each poem. A sample discussion guideline is provided for a sample of poems from the literature selection. You will need to provide enough poems that each student has a turn to read a poem aloud.)

Poetry Analysis

(Ask a student to read aloud the poem "Lulu, Lulu, I've a Lilo" from page 11.) Sometimes poets play with words in their poems. Charlotte Pomerantz, in her poem "Lulu, Lulu, I've a Lilo", has used her poem to teach the listener four words from the Samoan language. Listen again to the poem. (Have student read poem a second time.)

(Ask a student to read aloud the poem "Where Do These Words Come From?" from page 11.) This is another poem in which the author plays with words. Why do you think the poet chose these words for his poem? (Call on a student. Idea: *They are all English words that are derived from Native American languages.*) What is unique about the poem? (Call on a student. Idea: *It is a list of words.*) Do some of the lines of this poem rhyme? (Signal.) *Yes.* What is the rhyming pattern of this poem? (Call on a student. Idea: *Each pair of lines rhymes.*)

(Ask a student to read aloud the poem "Night Creature" from page 121. Write the word **glare-y** on the chalkboard.) In this poem Lilian Moore plays with words another way. (Point to the word glare-y.) Is the word **glare-y** usually spelled with a hyphen? (Signal.) *No.* The poet used the hyphen to encourage the reader to pause before reading the **-y.** How does this affect the poem? (Call on a student. Idea: *It affects the rhythm and pace of the poem.*)

Sometimes a poet invents words when he or she writes poetry. As you listen to the poem, think about which words are the invented words in this poem. (Ask a student to read aloud the poem "Eletelephony" on page 108.) What are the invented words in this poem? (Call on different students. Ideas: *Telephon; telephant; elephone; telephunk; telephee; elephop; and telephong.*)

(Ask a student to read aloud the poem "Stopping by Woods on a Snowy Evening" from Page 36.) What is the mood conveyed in this poem? (Call on different students. Ideas: *Anticipation, awe, wonderment with nature.*) How does this poem make you feel? Explain why it makes you feel this way. (Call on different students. Accept reasonable responses.)

(Ask a student to read aloud the poem "who knows if the moon's" on page 120. Write e.e. cummings' name and line 4 on the chalkboard.) e.e. cummings's poetry demonstrates another way that poets use language and words. e.e. cummings does not use capital letters or punctuation the conventional way. (Have available other poetry from e.e. cummings for the students to examine during the follow-up activity.)

(Ask a student to read aloud the poem "If We Walked on Our Hands" on page 105.) The length of lines varies in poetry from long to short. (Show students a copy of the poem.) What kinds of lines does this poem have? (Call on a student. Idea: *Both long and short lines.*) Beatrice Schenk de Regniers uses many of the techniques of poetry in this poem. Does this poem have a rhyming pattern? (Signal.) *Yes.* Tell us about the rhyming pattern in this poem. (Call on a student. Idea: *Lines two and four rhyme.* Write the word **sit-u-a-tion** on the chalkboard.) What other poem used hyphens within words? (Call on a student. Idea: *Night Creature.*) Sometimes poems have repeating parts at the end of each verse. What lines repeat in this poem? (Call on a student. *Student repeats the last five lines of each verse.*) How do the repeating lines affect the poem? (Call on a student. Ideas: *They affect the rhythm of the poem. They make it like the chorus of a song.*) What mood does this poem create? (Call on different students. Ideas: *Humor, having fun, joy, laughter.*)

Figurative language is used by poets to paint a picture in the minds of readers and listeners. Listen to this poem and see if you hear an example of figurative language. (Ask a student to read aloud the poem "Firefly" on page 129.) What part of the poem is figurative language? (Call on a student. Idea: *You would twinkle like a star.*)

What do we call this type of figurative language? (Call on a student. Idea: *A simile.* Ask a student to read aloud the poem "Mirrorment" on page 132.) What kind of figurative language is this whole poem? (Call on a student. Idea: *A metaphor.*)

Some poems appeal to our senses and feelings. Listen to this poem and think about to which one of your senses the poet is appealing. (Ask a student to read aloud "Night Creature" on page 121.) Which of our senses does Lilian Moore want us to use when we read or listen to her poem? (Signal.) *Hearing.*

Something that is **abstract** is not an actual object. It is a thought or a feeling that may be hard to put into words. Poets often use their poetry to explain an abstract feeling or thought. (Ask a student to read aloud "Poem" on page 116.) What abstract thought or feeling is Langston Hughes telling about in his poem? (Call on a student. Idea: *The feeling of loss when a beloved friend leaves.*)

The opposite of abstract is **concrete.** Poetry about real objects is considered to be concrete. (Ask a student to read aloud the poem "Tails" on page 70.) Is the subject of this poem abstract or concrete? (Signal.) *Concrete.* Explain why. (Call on a student. Idea: *It tells about the object* **tails**.)

Dialect is how people from a certain part of a country speak. The last poem that will be read has two words that A.A. Milne used that are written in dialect. A.A. Milne was born in England. His dialect of English is slightly different than American English. Listen to the poem and see if you can hear the two words that are written in dialect. (Ask a student to read aloud the poem "Furry Bear" on page 22.) What two words are written in dialect? (Call on different students. *Snew and friz.*) What does the word **snew** mean? (Signal.) *Snow.* What does the word **friz** mean? (Signal.) *Froze.* Why do you think A.A. Milne used dialect for these two words? (Call on a student. Idea: *It helped him rhyme some of the lines in his poem.*)

Activity

Reading/Research/Writing
Poetry/Speaking/Listening/Illustrating

Title: *The Great Poetry Search*

Time required: 30 minutes

Materials required: BLM 11, one copy for each student
A variety of books, magazines, journals audiotapes, videotapes with poetry selections, Internet

Procedure

1. (Give each student a copy of BLM 11. Scatter various poetry materials around the classroom.) Today you are going on a great poetry search. You have learned about many of the characteristics of poetry. You will search through the materials that are set out to find poems that match each clue on your sheet. See how many examples you can find for each clue. Ready, set, go!

2. (After 20 minutes of searching, call the class together to share the results of their searches. Ask students to raise their hands if they found the same poem to match the clue. Have students give specific examples of why the poem they found matches the clue.)

3. (Have students write and illustrate a poem in the style of choice. Encourage them to use as many of the techniques that have been discussed as they can. After final copies and illustrations are completed, have students practice reading their poems to a partner.)

4. (Have a class poetry reading by the various student authors. Have the poet lead classmates through a brief discussion of his or her poem following the discussion guidelines from the literature lesson.)

Technology

Students may find additional poems on the Internet. Have students type the final copies of their poems using a word-processing program, experimenting with different styles and sizes of font to enhance their poetry. Graphics and animation programs may be used in the illustration process. Students may also use simple moviemaking programs to illustrate poetry.

Reader Preference

Think about the various poems you have heard. Write a paragraph that answers the following questions. (Write the questions on the chalkboard or on an overhead.) Which poem did you enjoy the most? Explain why. Did any of the techniques that we discussed add to your enjoyment of the poem? Which did you prefer—the poetry in the print materials or the poetry written by your classmates? How did the presentation of the poem affect your preference?

ADDITIONAL LITERATURE

Following are some additional titles that your students may enjoy during and following this lesson.

The Rime of the Ancient Mariner by Samuel Taylor Coleridge

The Cremation of Sam McGee by Robert W. Service

Shadow by Marcia Brown

The Great Poetry Search

Find an example of poetry that matches each clue. Support each of your examples with a reason or by copying the part of the poem that shows why the poem you have chosen matches the clue.

Find a poem:

1. Where the poet plays with words: _____

How does the poet play with words? _____

_____

2. That is a list: _____

What kind of list is it? _____

3. That has lines that rhyme: _____

Describe the rhyming pattern found in this poem. _____

_____

4. With invented words: _____

Write the invented words that are found in this poem. _____

_____

5. That sets a certain mood: _____

What is the mood of this poem? _____

6. That does not follow the conventions of language such as correct punctuation and

capitalization: _____

Who wrote this poem? _____

What conventions are not followed? _____

© SRA/McGraw-Hill. Permission is granted to reproduce this page for classroom use.

7. With both long and short lines: _____

   With short lines: _____

   With long lines: _____

8. With repeating parts: _____

   Copy the part that repeats: _____

9. With figurative language: _____

   What kind of figurative language is used in this poem? _____

   Copy the part of the poem that is figurative language: _____

   _____

10. Which appeals to one or more of your senses: _____

    To what sense or senses does this poem appeal? _____

11. That is abstract: _____

    Explain why this poem is abstract. _____

    _____

12. That is concrete: _____

    Explain why this poem is concrete. _____

    _____

13. That uses dialect: _____

    Give an example of the dialect that is used in this poem. _____

© SRA/McGraw-Hill. Permission is granted to reproduce this page for classroom use.

Lesson 12

Language Skill Development
Using Present, Past, and Future Perfect Verb Tenses

Time Required: 15 minutes

Preparation: Write the following sentences on the chalkboard or an overhead transparency:

1. Carl _____ (finish writing) his story, so now we can read it.
2. Carl _____ (finish writing) his story, so we read it in class yesterday.
3. Carl _____ (finish writing) his story by the end of the day.
4. Ulani _____ (picked) some tomatoes, so let's make a salad.
5. Ulani _____ (picked) some tomatoes, so we made a salad.
6. Ulani _____ (picked) some tomatoes by dinnertime.

Write the following verb constructions and rules on a piece of chart paper:

1. **Jerome <u>has finished</u> doing his homework, so we can come over.**
   (Present perfect → action completed at this exact time.)

2. **Jerome <u>had finished</u> doing his homework, so his friends came over.**
   (Past perfect → action completed before another past action.)

3. **Jerome <u>will have finished</u> doing his homework by the time his friends come over.** (Future perfect → action will be completed before something else happens in the future.)

Let's review what you have learned about the present, past, and future perfect verb tenses. The perfect verb tense is used when you want to talk about an action that was finished before another action. (Point to the sentences on the chalkboard.) In these sentences, two things are happening. One is that Jerome is doing his homework. The other is that his friends are coming over to see him.

(Point to the first sentence on the chart.) Read the first sentence aloud. (Signal.) *Jerome has finished doing his homework, so we can come over.* What is the first action? (Call on a student. Idea: *Jerome has finished doing his homework.*) Has the first action just been completed at this moment? (Signal.) *Yes.* Jerome has just finished doing his homework at this exact moment, so this example uses the present perfect tense.

(Point to the second sentence on the chart.) Read the second sentence aloud. (Signal.) *Jerome had finished doing his homework, so his friends came over.* What is the first action? (Call on a student. Idea: *Jerome had finished doing his homework.*) Has the first action already been completed before something else happened? (Signal.) *Yes.* Jerome finished doing his homework before his friends came over, so this example uses the past perfect tense.

(Point to the third sentence on the chart.) Read the third sentence aloud. (Signal.) *Jerome will have finished doing his homework by the time his friends come over.* What will be the first action? (Call on a student. Idea: *Jerome will have finished doing his homework.*) Will the first action be completed in the future before something else happens? (Signal.) *Yes.* Jerome will have finished doing his homework before his friends come over, so this example uses the future perfect tense.

(Point to the sentences on the chalkboard.) You will copy each of these sentences with the correct perfect verb tense for each group of words that is in the parentheses. Use the sentences and information from the chart to help you decide how to state the verb correctly.

Media Lesson

**Note: Activity One is introductory to the literature selection.

Introductory Activity

Speaking/Map Reading

Title: *Where's It From*

> **Time Required:** 20 minutes
>
> **Materials Required:** A world map hung on a bulletin board, Several colored pushpins for inserting into the map

Procedure

1. During the next few days, you will be reading books and articles about child labor and the rights of children. To begin, pair up with a partner and check the labels of your clothes to find out where they were made. Don't forget to look at the labels in your shoes as well. (**Point to the world map on the wall.**) When you find where an article of clothing is made, come up to the map, and push a pin (**show students location of pins**) into the country where the clothing was made. (**Allow students time to identify clothing origin and locate each country on the world map.**)

2. (**Assign several different students the task of counting the number of pins in each country and writing the tally on the chalkboard.**) Which country manufactured the most clothing? (**Signal.**) (**Students identify the country with the highest number of pins.**) What other countries manufactured our clothes? (**Call on different students. Students identify other countries that manufactured clothes.**)

3. Many of the things that we buy are made by children in other countries, some younger than you. The book we will read during the next activity tells about the lives of children who were forced to work in factories at a very young age.

Literature

Kids at Work: Lewis Hine and the Crusade Against Child Labor

By Russell Freedman

Materials Required: The text of each chapter of *Kids at Work*, one copy for each group.

(Hold up a copy of *Kids at Work*.) This is the book that we will be reading today. (Point to the title.) Read the title of the book. (Call on a student. *Kids at Work*.) Sometimes a book has a subtitle under the main title. What is the subtitle of this book? (Call on a student. *Lewis Hine and the Crusade Against Child Labor*. Point to the author's name on the cover.) Who is the author of this book? (Call on a student. *Russell Freedman*.)

This book is full of the photographs that Lewis Hine took of children working in mines, canneries, and factories. Who took the photographs in this book? (Signal.) *Lewis Hine*.

(Divide the class into seven groups. Assign one chapter to each group.) You are all going to become experts in one chapter of this book. Your job will be to read the chapter carefully, and then take notes of the most important information. (Students may each read the chapter independently or take turns reading paragraphs from their chapters aloud to one another.)

Activity One

Note-taking/Writing a Summary/Listening/Speaking

> **Title: *Presenting Information in a Learning Jigsaw***
> **Time Required:** 30 minutes
> **Materials Required:** Appropriate copies of BLM 12A – 12H, one copy for every student in each group

Procedure

1. You will summarize the information that you learned in your chapter on note cards. (Distribute the appropriate BLM to every student in each group.) Reread the chapter with your group and write down the information you learned in the correct

spaces on the summary sheet. (You may wish to have more able students independently collect and summarize information without the cues of the note cards. However, these students should prepare a note card from which to speak.)

2. After each person in your group has completed his or her summary sheet, one student from each group will join another group. Each new group will contain a representative from each chapter of the book. (Give students sufficient time to reorganize into new groupings.)

3. Every student who learned about Chapter One will now share what he or she learned with the rest of the group. You are the expert on the information from Chapter One. Read the information you collected on your summary sheet. Remember to look up at your audience and to speak clearly so that everyone in the group can hear you. Members of your group may ask you questions about the information you presented.

4. When person one has finished presenting the information from Chapter One, the person who is the expert for Chapter Two will present. (Repeat process until all chapters in the book have been presented.)

Activity Two

Listening/Note Taking/Writing

> ### Title: *United Nations Declaration of the Rights of the Child*
>
> **Materials Required:** A copy of the UN Declaration of the Rights of the Child BLM 12H, one copy for each student

Procedure

1. Today, I will read you the United Nations Declaration of the Rights of the Child. Raise your hand if you can tell us what the United Nations is. (Call on a student. Idea: *An organization made up of representatives of many different countries who meet and discuss global issues that affect every nation on Earth.*) Raise your hand if you can predict what you think some of the rights of children are. (Call on different students. Accept several responses.)

2. I will read you the United Nations Declaration of the Rights of the Child twice. The first time I read it, all you have to do is listen carefully. The second time I read it, you will summarize what you think are the most important parts of this document using your own words. (Read the UN Declaration of the Rights of the Child aloud once.)

3. (Distribute BLM 12H, one copy to each student.) Listen carefully as I reread each part of the document. You will summarize what the most important points are to you for each principle, using your own words. (Read the UN Declaration of the Rights of the Child a second time, ensuring that students have adequate time to write their responses between sections.)

4. Do you think that these are fair rules for adults and children? (Call on different students. Accept two or three responses.) Raise your hand if you can think of a situation in your life where these rules apply to you. (Call on different students. Accept several responses.)

Activity Three

Researching/Evaluating Media

> **Title: *Recognizing Propaganda in Advertising***
> **Time Required:** 40 minutes
> **Materials Required:** A variety of magazines which feature clothing and shoe advertisements

Procedure

1. Companies rely on advertisements to ensure that people buy their products. Advertisements are designed to persuade and convince people that they want or need to buy a product. What are advertisements designed to do? (Signal.) *Persuade and convince people that they want or need to buy a product.*

2. Companies often use persuasive language to convince you to buy their products. They tell you how good a product is, or that it is better than another product. Sometimes companies don't use language to persuade. Instead, they use pictures or images of how the product could change your life or make you a happier, more popular, or more attractive person.

3. Raise your hand if you can tell us of some of the ways companies use pictures or images to try to persuade you that you will be happier, more popular, or more attractive if you buy their products. (Call on different students. Ideas: *Car ads in male-targeted magazines featuring beautiful women in the passenger seat or on the hood; models smiling and having a good time drinking or wearing products; beautiful, slim, and athletic young men and women in designer clothes.*)

4. Raise your hand if you can give us an example of different kinds of advertisements that you see every day. (Call on different students. Ideas: *television commercials, magazines ads, billboards, signs on buses and trucks, posters in bus shelters.*)

5. (Distribute magazines to students.) Independently or in a group, spend some time looking for clothing and shoe advertisements. (Give students enough time to look for ads.) In your notebook, write down the name of the company, what kind of shoes or clothing it is advertising, and what methods it uses to persuade people to buy its brand of clothes or shoes.

6. What methods do companies use to persuade you to buy their products? (Call on different students. Ideas: *Celebrities like basketball players and famous actors wearing or using products, beautiful models, young models.*) From what you've learned about how companies market their products, what would you conclude

are the values that are the most important in our society today? (Call on different students. Ideas: *Beauty, youth, leading an exciting and fun life, power, wealth, friendship.*)

Technology

Now that you have looked at some advertisements, research where the products are made and by whom. Some places that were using child labor in 1998 include South Asia, Bangladesh, India, Pakistan, and Nepal. It is often difficult to discover which companies manufacture clothes using child labor. Use the Internet or your school library to find more information on clothing companies and child labor.

(Have students find additional information on the Internet on child labor and clothing companies who use it to manufacture their products, and tell them to take notes on what they find. Some places to start may include UNICEF, Anti-Slavery International, Human Rights Watch/Asia, BLLF, and the NCLC.)

ADDITIONAL LITERATURE:

Following are some additional titles that your students may enjoy during and following the lesson.

ADDITIONAL LITERATURE

Following are some additional titles that your students may enjoy during and following this lesson.

Iqbal Masih and the Crusaders Against Child Slavery by Susan Kuklin.

"Child Labor in Pakistan" in *Atlantic Monthly* by Jonathan Silvers (February 1996).

"The Short, Tragic Life of Iqbal Masih" in *Harper's Bazaar* by Trudie Styler (February 1996).

"Children of a Lesser God" in *Harper's Bazaar* by Mark Schapiro (April 1996).

Summary Sheet for Chapter One of *Kids at Work*

America's _____ was expanding, so _____, _____, and

_____ needed plenty of _____.

More than _____ under _____ of age worked _____ hours a

day or more _____ days a week.

Where did children work? _____

What were the conditions like? _____

Children were _____ by _____ in their faces.

By _____ many Americans were calling child labor _____ and

were demanding _____. They argued that _____ deprived

children of _____ and robbed them of _____.

_____ said that children have the right to _____ .

What did child labor promise a future of? _____

Who was Lewis Hine? _____

What did he do to fight child labor? _____

Factory owners didn't want _____ nosing around their plants, and many

_____ were _____, _____, and _____. Hine

was _____ enough to _____, snapping scenes

that _____

Why were Americans shocked? _____

© SRA/McGraw-Hill. Permission is granted to reproduce this page for classroom use.

Summary Sheet for Chapter Two of *Kids at Work*

Why were adult workers replaced by children in 1893? _____.

_____ was a _____ who encouraged Lewis to _____

_____. Frank Manny invited Lewis to _____ _____as a

teacher of _____ and _____.

Lewis Hine took up _____ to document _____.

Describe Lewis' equipment: _____

Why did Manny want Hine to photograph immigrant families? _____

_____

Lewis started working for _____ who were _____ in the

_____ of New York and _____.

A _____ old girl made _____ paper flowers a day for _____
cents.

A family making roses worked from _____ to _____ or_____ at night, making

$_____ a day.

Hine was _____ by the _____ and _____ he witnessed

in the tenements. In 1908, the _____ offered Lewis a job as

_____ in its campaign to _____.

© SRA/McGraw-Hill. Permission is granted to reproduce this page for classroom use.

Summary Sheet for Chapter Three of *Kids at Work*

Lewis traveled from the _____ of Maine to the _____ of Texas

taking pictures of _____, listening to _____ and reporting on

_____. His goal was to _____ to the horrors of _____.

He wanted to _____.

Hine wasn't worried by children who _____, but the exploitation of kids as

_____Why were children hired? _____

Why weren't the child-labor laws enforced? _____

The _____ was founded in _____ and was a _____

organization that believed a _____, _____, _____

childhood was the _____ of all children. The _____ wanted to ban

_____ under _____ in most occupations, and under _____ in

_____ trades like _____. What four other things

did the NCLC demand? _____

_____

Why couldn't Hine get into factories? _____

How did he take pictures anyway? _____

How did he document his pictures? _____

© SRA/McGraw-Hill. Permission is granted to reproduce this page for classroom use.

Summary Sheet for Chapter Four of _Kids at Work_

_____ were big offenders, and _____ in every _____ mill workers

were between the ages of _____ and _____. Workers younger than _____

weren't _____.

Why did children quit school early or never go? _____

Describe the work of children in cotton mills: _____

_____

How long did a spinner work? _____ How many days a week? _____

If kids weren't careful, they could _____ or be _____. The

_____ rate for _____ in the mills was _____ as high as

it was for _____. Windows were kept closed and mill workers developed

_____, _____, and other _____ because the

_____, _____ air was filled with _____ and

_____ that made it hard to _____.

Why weren't child-labor laws enforced? _____

What other industry employed entire families? _____

The worker camps were _____, had no _____ and were infested

with _____ and _____. Work in canning sheds began at

_____ in the morning.

Why was shrimp harmful? _____

What other hazards did children face in the canneries? _____

Why did cannery owners want kids to work? _____

© SRA/McGraw-Hill. Permission is granted to reproduce this page for classroom use.

Summary Sheet for Chapter Five of *Kids at Work*

In Pennsylvania, the biggest _____ state, thousands of _____ and

_____ year-old boys worked legally in _____. Thousands of

younger boys, some of them only _____ or _____, worked

_____.

What was a coal breaker? _____

If a boy _____ and _____ into the _____, he could be

_____ or _____. _____ boys died while Hine visited the

mine. A _____ armed with a _____ rapped on the heads of boys

who, in his opinion, _____. Many breaker boys suffered from _____.

When the boys were _____, they began work in the _____ where there

was a threat of _____ and _____.

What other industry did boys work in? _____

What were some hazards? _____

Why did the boys work at night? _____

Because of _____ and _____ work conditions, glass-making

employees had a life expectancy of only _____ to _____ years.

© SRA/McGraw-Hill. Permission is granted to reproduce this page for classroom use.

Summary Sheet for Chapter Six of *Kids at Work*

People were often _____ and _____ when they saw

_____ of _____ _____ working in _____,

_____, and _____. Yet young children at work _____

received _____.

What work did city kids do? _____

_____

Some youngsters Hine _____ had been _____ on

_____ _____ since they were _____ or _____ years old.

They received no _____ or _____, and took the _____

of any papers they couldn't _____.

Many _____ lived in _____, never _____, and had no

_____.

Why didn't people object to kids working on farms? _____

What were the harsh facts? _____

What were living conditions like? _____

Many _____ workers were _____ or members of other

_____, and in some places, were denied _____ and _____.

Why were ignorance and illiteracy widespread among young farmhands? _____

_____

Cotton-picking was called _____, and was a _____ and

_____ job.

How much could a four-year-old pick? _____ A five-year-old? _____

What were hazards of sugarbeet pulling and topping? _____

© SRA/McGraw-Hill. Permission is granted to reproduce this page for classroom use.

BLM 12G

Summary Sheet for Chapter Seven of *Kids at Work*

Hine's photos _____ what many had _____. They stood as

_____ that America was _____ its children. "These pictures

_____," the _____ declared, "and prove that _____."

What three things were Hine's photos meant to do? _____

_____

The photos became a _____ in the _____

against _____.

What special assignment did Hine accept in 1918? _____

After _____ the horrors of _____, Hine wanted to focus on the

_____, on its _____ and _____. His major project in the

1920s was called _____, which were _____ of _____

and _____. In 1930, Hine began a daring assignment photographing the

step-by-step _____ of _____.

Why did Hine die poor? _____

Why is he considered a master photographer today? _____

© SRA/McGraw-Hill. Permission is granted to reproduce this page for classroom use.

Summary Sheet for the UN Declaration of the Rights of the Child

Why do children need special rights? _____

_____

What does the General Assembly proclaim? _____

Principle 1: _____

Principle 2: _____

Principle 3: _____

Principle 4: _____

Principle 5: _____

Principle 6: _____

_____

Principle 7: _____

_____

Principle 8: _____

Principle 9: _____

_____

Principle 10: _____

© SRA/McGraw-Hill. Permission is granted to reproduce this page for classroom use.

Lesson 13

Language Skill Development

Listening/Writing

Title: *Using a Colon after a Salutation*
Time required: 20 minutes
Preparation: Write the following on the chalkboard or overhead transparency:

Castle Rock Middle School
46 Brown Street
Freemont City, MN 80941

April 12, 2001

Buns Bakery
465 Wheat Avenue
Freemont City, MN 80943

Dear Sir or Madam:

Our biology class is holding a school fundraiser to buy ten new microscopes. We have been asking local businesses if they would like to make any contributions to the Spring Fling Fair that our class is holding on Friday, May 2nd. There will be a bake sale and cake raffle to help raise money, and we were wondering if you would be interested in donating a cake to be raffled.

Thank you for considering our request. We appreciate the support that you provide to our school and to our community.

Sincerely,

Lia Potter
Student

Today we will review the format for writing a business letter. When you write a business letter, the first thing you write is the return address. (Point to the return address.) A return address is the address to which the person you are writing will mail his or her reply. Read the return address. (Call on a student. *Castle Rock Middle School, 46 Brown Street, Freemont City, Minnesota, 80941.*)

(Point to the date.) What did I write next? (Signal.) *The date of the letter.*

(Point to the inside address.) This is called the inside address. Read the inside address. (Call on a student. *Buns Bakery, 465 Wheat Avenue, Freemont City, Minnesota, 80943.*) What does the inside address tell? (Call on a student. *Where the letter is being sent.*)

(Point to the salutation.) The salutation is the name of the person to whom you are writing. What is the name of the person to whom you are writing called? (Signal.) *The salutation.* The salutation usually begins with the word **Dear,** followed by the person's name. When you don't know the name of the person who owns the company, you use the formal language **Dear Sir or Madam.** (Point to the salutation of the letter.) What is the salutation of this letter? (Signal.) *Dear Sir or Madam.*

After you write **Dear** and the person's name, the correct punctuation mark for the salutation of a business letter is a colon. (Draw a colon on the chalkboard.) Is there a colon after **Dear Sir or Madam** in this letter? (Signal.) *Yes.*

(Point to the body of the letter.) This is the body of the letter. Read the body of the letter to yourselves. (Give students sufficient time to silently read the letter.) What does the body of this business letter tell? (Call on different students. Idea: *It is a request for a cake. It thanks the business for considering the request and for its support.*)

(Point to the closing.) What do we call this part of the letter? (Signal.) *The closing.* Often people write **Sincerely,** or **Yours truly** as a closing. The first letter of the closing is always capitalized. (Point to the closing of the letter.) What is the closing of this letter? (Signal.) *Sincerely.* Does **Sincerely** begin with a capital letter? (Signal.) *Yes.*

What punctuation mark goes after the closing? (Signal.) *A comma.*

(Point to the last two lines of the letter.) The letter writer skipped four lines and then wrote her name. What did the letter writer write under Lia's name? (Call on a student. *Her title.*)

(Point to the space for a signature.) What will the letter writer put in this space? (Call on a student. *Her signature.*) What is a signature? (Call on a student. *It's when you write your name with a pen or pencil.*)

(Write on the chalkboard: **Mrs. Johnson, Mr. Pedro Lupez, Ms. Anita Redford.**) In your notebooks, practice writing these names as salutations. Remember to use correct capitalization and punctuation.

Literature

The Great Kapok Tree: A Tale of the Amazon Rain Forest

by Lynne Cherry

Examining the Book

> **Note:** *The Great Kapok Tree* is a rich source of information about tropical rain forests. Although it is now dated, the information in the book is startling and still relevant. Close attention to the inside front cover pages will reveal the extent to which rain forests had been destroyed up to roughly 1990. The border on those pages displays and names rain forest animals and birds. The introduction which precedes the main title page is brief but is a convincing argument. Following the main title page is a dedication to Chico Mendes, a historical figure associated with rain forest preservation. Your class may wish to research Mendes and other such figures in books, in an electronic encyclopedia, or on the Internet as a class project.

Reading the Book

The reading may be preceded by a discussion of vocabulary and terminology that is specific to the rain forest like: **canopy, understory,** and **Yanomamo tribe.** Following a discussion of the vocabulary, read the book with minimal interruptions.

Activity One

Reading/Listening/Speaking/Performing in a role

> **Title:** *Radio Play: The Great Kapok Tree: A Tale of the Amazon Rain Forest*
>
> **Materials Required:** A recorded example of a radio play from the twentieth century (Dramatic serials such as *The Shadow* or *The Green Lantern* are appropriate for this age level as is H.G. Wells's *War of the Worlds*.)
>
> One copy of *The Great Kapok Tree* for each student
>
> One copy of the radio play script for each student (roles to be assigned by teacher) (BLM 13A)
>
> A tape recorder for preserving the radio play as a performance

Procedure

1. (Discuss the concept of a radio play.) Radio was a communication device extensively used prior to the introduction of television. Like books, which require the active imaginations of readers to create mental images of characters and settings, radio plays depended on the listening skills and imaginations of the audience to be successful.

2. (Have students listen to an excerpt of a recording of a radio play—suggestions are given above but other selections may be appropriate. Ask your students to identify the elements of radio play (a compelling story, strong characters, careful enunciation, music, and sound effects) that inspire imagination. Draw their attention to the advertisements given by the program's sponsor(s) if you choose to include sponsor advertisements or commercials as a part of the radio play.)

3. (Point to the boxed-in passage on the first page of the story.) Each passage in this book is enclosed in a box. Use your pencil to number the boxes lightly in pencil in the bottom center of each box, starting with the first page of the story. The radio play will refer to sentences within those boxes. The boxes should be numbered from 1 — 16. The introduction prior to the title page will be referred to as "the brief introduction." This box should not be numbered.

4. (Assign roles to individuals and small groups as necessary according to the cast list provided. Where specific sounds are required, take suggestions from the class and choose the best suggestions for use in the play.)

5. (Rehearse the radio play until students can perform it fluently and with dramatic expression, making suggestions and adjustments as it proceeds.)

6. (Perform the radio play and record it. The radio play may be shared with other classes in a variety of ways: recorded onto a tape and played to others or over the school PA system. Listening to the radio play could prove to be an excellent listening/sketching exercise for other classes.)

ADDITIONAL LITERATURE

Following are some additional titles that your students may enjoy during and following this lesson.

Elephant Woman by Laurence Pringle

Ecology for Every Kid by Janice VanCleave

Lifetimes by David L. Rice

The Great Kapok Tree: A Tale of the Amazon Rain Forest

written and illustrated by Lynne Cherry

adapted for radio play by Rick Williams

Cast and Sounds (assignments as appropriate to your class)

All characters will need a copy of the book *The Great Kapok Tree* to read aloud where direct quotes are taken from the book. Additional parts (e.g., the Announcer and Sponsor parts, if used) may be read directly from these lesson pages.

Announcer:

Narrator 1:

Narrator 2:

Narrator 3:

Narrator 4:

Man:

Boa Constrictor:

Bee:

Four Monkeys:

Toucan:

Small Tree Frog:

Jaguar:

Four Tree Porcupines:

Unstriped Anteater:

Three-toed Sloth:

Yanamamo Child:

Sound Effects

Rainforest animals and sounds: Everyone

Footsteps coming closer (two men):

Whacking and Chopping:

Slithering:

Hum of the forest:

Animals (make your own sound from the script):

Man breathing in quickly, startled:

Man picking up something heavy:

Man breathing in:

Man dropping something heavy:

One man's footsteps walking away and becoming quieter:

© SRA/McGraw-Hill. Permission is granted to reproduce this page for classroom use.

The Great Kapok Tree: A Tale of the Amazon Rain Forest

Announcer: Good morning (or afternoon) ladies, gentlemen and children of all ages! Welcome to (your school's name) School's "Theatre of the Air" production of *The Great Kapok Tree*. Today we are featuring the talents of (teacher's name)'s Grade (grade number) class. We truly hope that you will enjoy this morning's (afternoon's) performance.

A silent pause.

Note to the teacher: If you wish to combine a study of media and advertising with this production, you may insert a "message from our sponsor" here. The message should be followed by the silent pause.

Narrator 1: Read first six sentences of the brief introduction that precedes the main title page.

Narrator 2: Read the remainder of the brief introduction.

Everyone: Rainforest sounds, the sounds of your animals.

Narrator 1: READ BOX 1 SENTENCE 1. [Sound effect of the footsteps of two men walking] READ THE REST OF BOX 1.

Narrator 2: READ BOX 2, SENTENCE 1

Everyone (watch for teacher's directions): **READ BOX 2, SENTENCE 2 (Whacking sound effect):**

Narrator 2: READ BOX 2, SENTENCES 3 AND 4.

Everyone (watch for teacher's directions) **READ BOX 2, SENTENCE 5 (Chopping sound effect):**

Narrator 2: READ BOX 2, SENTENCE 6:

Man: *"Boy, this is hard work!"*

Everyone (watch for teacher's directions): **READ BOX 2, SENTENCE 7 (Whacking, chopping sound effect):**

Narrator 2: READ BOX 2, SENTENCE 8:

Man (huffing and puffing): *"Whew, I need a rest!"*

© SRA/McGraw-Hill. Permission is granted to reproduce this page for classroom use.

Narrator 2: READ BOX 2, SENTENCES 8 AND 9: [Make a soft humming sound during the reading of sentence 9]

Narrator 3: READ BOX 3, SENTENCES 1, 2, and 3: [Make a slithering sound during the reading of sentence 2]

Boa Constrictor (with a hissing sound): **READ BOX 3, SENTENCES 4, 5, AND 6:**

Narrator 3: READ BOX 4, SENTENCE 1 TO THE COLON

Bee: READ BOX 4, FINISHING SENTENCE 1 AND CONTINUING TO THE END OF THE BOX:

Narrator 3: READ BOX 5, SENTENCE 1, THEN SENTENCE 2 TO THE COLON:

Monkeys (chattering): **READ BOX 5, FINISHING SENTENCE 2 AND CONTINUE TO THE END OF THE BOX:**

Narrator 3: READ BOX 6, SENTENCE 1:

Toucan (sqawking): **READ BOX 6 FROM SENTENCE 2 TO THE END:**

Narrator 4: READ BOX 7, TO THE COLON IN SENTENCE 2:

Tree Frog (in a small, squeaky voice): **READ BOX 7, FINISHING SENTENCE 2 AND CONTINUING TO THE END:**

Narrator 4: READ BOX 8 TO THE COLON IN SENTENCE 4:

Jaguar (growling): **READ BOX 8, FINISHING SENTENCE 4 AND CONTINUING TO THE END:**

Narrator 4: READ BOX 9, TO THE COLON IN SENTENCE 1:

Four Tree Porcupines (whispering): **READ BOX 9, FINISHING SENTENCE 1 AND CONTINUING TO THE END:**

Narrator 4: READ BOX 10, TO THE COLON IN SENTENCE 2:

Unstriped Anteater (speaking in a voice that <u>you</u> think sounds like an anteater): **READ BOX 10, FINISHING SENTENCE 2 AND CONTINUING TO THE END:**

Narrator 4: READ BOX 11, TO THE COLON IN SENTENCE 3:

Three-toed Sloth (in a deep and lazy voice): **READ BOX 11, FINISHING SENTENCE 3 AND CONTINUING TO THE END:**

Narrator 4: READ BOX 12, TO THE COLON IN SENTENCE 2:

Yanomamo child (murmuring): **READ BOX 12, FINISHING SENTENCE 2**

© SRA/McGraw-Hill. Permission is granted to reproduce this page for classroom use.

Narrator 4: READ BOX 13 AND 14 [Make the sound of breathing in quickly, sounding startled in the first sentence]:

Narrators 1, 2, 3, and 4 (slowly): **READ BOX 15 TO THE END [Make the sound effect of picking up something heavy in the first sentence]; [Make the sound of taking in a deep breath in the second sentence]; [Pause briefly at the end of the third sentence]:**

Narrators 1, 2, 3, and 4: READ BOX 16 [Make the sound effect of something heavy dropping and hitting the ground in sentence 2]; [Make the sound effect of the footsteps of one man getting farther away and quieter].

A silent pause.

Announcer: Ladies, gentlemen, and children of all ages, we hope you have enjoyed (your school's name) School's radio play rendition of Lynne Cherry's *The Great Kapok Tree*. We hope you will join us again for future broadcasts. Until then, the actors bid you a fond farewell!

(Another message from a sponsor would be appropriate at this juncture, if desired.)

© SRA/McGraw-Hill. Permission is granted to reproduce this page for classroom use.

Language Skill Development

Punctuating Dialogue

Time Required: 20 minutes

Preparation: Write the following sentences on the chalkboard or on an overhead transparency:

1. **Can you see me asked Joan**
2. **Felix yelled jump higher**
3. **I'm not hungry said Kenisha**
4. **His mother called out don't be late for class**
5. **Alberto said come over to my house**

Materials Required: A book containing an example of dialogue

Let's review what you already know about dialogue. The words that people say out loud in a story are called dialogue. What are the words that people say out loud in a story called? (Signal.) *Dialogue.* When you write dialogue, every word that is spoken out loud must be surrounded by quotation marks. (Show students an example of dialogue surrounded by quotation marks.)

The quotation marks that go in front of dialogue look like a pair of sixes. (Draw a set of opening quotation marks that look like sixes on the chalkboard.) The quotation marks that go after the dialogue look like a pair of nines. (Draw a set of closing quotation marks that look like nines on the chalkboard.)

(Write on the chalkboard: **You should try to run faster suggested Toby.**) Read this sentence aloud. (Signal.) *You should try to run faster suggested Toby.*

Raise your hand if you can tell us the dialogue in this sentence. (Call on a student. Idea: *You should try to run faster.*) You need to put a comma or another punctuation mark after what the speaker says. (Insert a comma after *faster.*)

The next thing you need to do is to put a pair of quotation marks at the beginning of the dialogue. (Put quotation marks before **You**.) Now you need to put quotation marks at the end of the dialogue. Quotation marks at the end of dialogue always go after the punctuation mark, so I will write in the quotation marks after the comma. (Put quotation marks after the comma.) What are quotation marks at the end of dialogue always put after? (Signal.) *The punctuation mark.* Let's read the sentence again now that it is punctuated properly. (Signal.) *"You should try to run faster," suggested Toby.*

(Write on the chalkboard: **Maria shouted look at all those stars.**) Read this sentence aloud. (Signal.) *Maria shouted look at all those stars.*

(Point to the words *Maria shouted.*) This part of the dialogue is called the **stem.** What is this part of the dialogue called? (Signal.) *The stem.* Raise your hand if you can tell us what punctuation mark goes at the end of the stem. (Call on a student. Idea: *A comma.* Ask student to come to the chalkboard to insert the comma.)

What is the dialogue in this sentence? (Call on a student. Idea: *Look at all those stars.*) The beginning of dialogue starts with a capital letter. (Erase the lower case **l** and replace it with a capital **L**.)

Raise your hand if you can tell us where to put the first set of quotation marks. (Call on a student. Idea: *Before **Look**.* Ask a student to come to the chalkboard and insert quotation marks before **Look.**)

How did Maria say her dialogue? Did she shout or did she whisper? (Signal.) *She shouted.* Raise your hand if you can tell us what punctuation mark we should use at the end of the dialogue. (Call on a student. *An exclamation mark.* Ask student to come up to the chalkboard and insert an exclamation mark at the end of the dialogue.)

Raise your hand if you can tell us where to put the second set of quotation marks. Remember, quotation marks that go at the end of dialogue are always put after the punctuation mark. (Call on a student. Idea: *After the exclamation mark.* Ask student to come to the chalkboard and insert quotation marks after the exclamation mark.) Let's read the sentence again now that it is punctuated properly. (Signal.) *Maria shouted, "Look at all those stars!"*

(Point to the sentences on the chalkboard or overhead transparency.) Rewrite each sentence in your notebook using the correct punctuation marks and capitalization.

Literature

The Most Beautiful Roof in the World: Exploring the Rainforest Canopy
by Kathryn Lasky

Materials required: A map of the world

Examining the Book

This is the next book that we are going to read and discuss. (Point to the title.) Read the title of the book. (Call on a student.) *The Most Beautiful Roof in the World.* Sometimes a book has a subtitle. (Point to the subtitle.) Read the subtitle of the book. (Call on a student. *Exploring the Rainforest Canopy.* Point to the author's name on the cover.) Who is the author of *The Most Beautiful Roof in the World*? (Call on a student. *Kathryn Lasky.* Point to the photographer's name on the cover.) Who took the photographs for *The Most Beautiful Roof in the World*? (Call on a student. *Christopher G. Knight.*)

Today's story tells the facts about a scientist named Meg Lowman who studies the rainforest. What is a story that tells facts called? (Signal.) *Nonfiction.* The genre of *The Most Beautiful Roof in the World* is photo essay. What is the genre of *The Most Beautiful Roof in the World*? (Signal.) *Photo essay.*

Reading the Book

I'm going to read this book aloud to you and show you the photographs. (Read the book with minimal interruptions—this ensures that the students hear the story in its entirety, thus helping them develop a better sense of story.)

OR

You may also wish to have your students take turns reading parts of the story aloud to classmates. Remind students of the conventions of being good readers and listeners.

(Occasionally you may find it beneficial to discuss parts of the story that are complicated or that have unfamiliar vocabulary. At the back of the book you will find a glossary of difficult words. Encourage students to check the illustrations, the structures of words, and context to help them decipher unknown words and their meanings.)

Literary Analysis

Where does this story take place? (Call on different students. Ideas: *In the Marie Selby Botanical Gardens in Sarasota, Florida; Blue Creek, located in Belize, Central America.* Show students the location of Sarasota, Florida, and Blue Creek, Belize, on a world map.)

When does this story take place? (Call on a student. Ideas: *In the present, during the past ten years.*) In a nonfiction book, it is often useful to know when the book was published. The year a book is published is written at the front of the book as the copyright date. (Show students the copyright page.) This book was copyrighted in 1997, so we know that the events in the book took place sometime before or in the year of 1997. If the book was published in 1997 and took place during the last ten years, when did Meg Lowman begin her rainforest research? (Call on a student. Idea: *1987.*)

What is Meg Lowman's job? (Call on a student. Idea: *To research the relationship between plants and insects in the rainforest canopy.*) How does she reach the rainforest canopy? (Call on a student. *She climbs tall trees and walks along treetop walkways.*)

Why did Meg decide to become a herbivory scientist—someone who researches leaves and plants eaten by insects? (Call on different students. Ideas: *She was always fascinated by the natural world; she was intrigued by two women environmentalists when she was ten.*)

What different insects and animals live in the rainforest canopy? (Call on different students. Ideas: *Ants, monkeys, lizards, macaws, emerald snakes, salamanders, butterflies.*)

What are some of the dangers of conducting research in the rainforest canopy? (Call on different students. Ideas: *Poisonous snakes; biting Army ants; tarantulas; baking heat; dangerous heights.*) What were some ways that Meg reached the canopy in other countries? (Call on different students. Idea: *On a huge floating raft moved around the treetops by a dirigible; on a huge construction crane standing in a gondola.*)

Why are James and Edward upset that Meg kills a "slingshot spider"? (Call on a student. Idea: *They are worried that it might be the last one.*) Remember that Meg Lowman has a special permit to capture or pick rare species of plants and insects. Do you think that she is a responsible environmentalist? (Call on different students. Accept two or three responses.)

Activity One

Reading/Writing/Speaking/Listening

> **Title: *Researching Ecological Issues***
>
> **Materials Required:** Index or note cards (ten per student)
>
> **Preparation:** Draw the brainstorming web below on the chalkboard or an overhead transparency:
>
> **Ecological Issues**
>
> **Air Pollution**
>
> **Endangered Species**   **Habitat Destruction**

Procedure

1. You are going to do a research project about an ecological issue. (Point to Endangered Species on the web.) Let's brainstorm a list of what we know about endangered species. Raise your hand if you can tell us about an endangered species that you know about. (Call on different students. Write responses on the chart as a web.)

2. (Point to Air Pollution on the web.) Let's brainstorm a list of what we know about air pollution. Raise your hand if you can tell us some things that contribute to air pollution. (Call on different students. Ideas: *Smog; cars; burning coal; factory emissions.* Write responses on the chart.)

3. (Point to Habitat Destruction on the web.) Let's brainstorm a list of what we know about habitat destruction. Raise your hand if you can tell us about how and why animal habitats are destroyed. (Call on different students. Ideas: *Building houses, condominiums and offices on old forest or meadow sites; cutting down rainforests to create farmland; clearcutting trees for wood production.* Write responses on the chart.)

4. (Ask students to make connections between different points to make a web.)

5. (Guide students through the following steps (Steps 6–16) of the research process. Give students sufficient time between each step of the process to ensure a high

quality of work. This research project may be completed as a whole class project, by a cooperative learning group, or as an individual project. As students work through their research, they will create a "research deck" on index cards or note cards. This deck will enable students to collect information in a format that is easily manipulated and revised without the tedium of rewriting. The decks may be used to facilitate note-taking, outlining and drafting. Final drafts may be handwritten or typed on a computer.)

6. (Point to the web that is on the chalkboard.) Choose an environmental issue that you would like to research as your topic. Think about questions that you want to ask about your topic. (Give each student 10 index or note cards.) Write one question on each of your note cards. This will be the start of your "research deck" of cards.

7. Organize your questions into groupings. Determine the topic heading for each of your groupings and write it on another note card. Put the heading at the beginning of the group of questions for that topic heading in your "research deck."

8. Now you are ready to identify sources for information. There are three types of sources. (Hold up one finger.) Firsthand sources. Making observations is an example of a firsthand source. What are other sources of firsthand information? (Call on different students. Idea: *Doing an experiment.* Hold up two fingers.) Secondhand sources. An interview is an example of a secondhand source. What are other sources of secondhand information? (Call on different students. Idea: *Talking to an expert.*) (Hold up three fingers.) Thirdhand sources. Written material or audiovisual media are examples of thirdhand sources. What are other sources of thirdhand information? (Call on different students. Idea: *The Internet, filmstrips, videos, books.*) Give me an example of where you would go to find each of the different kinds of sources. Be specific. (Call on different students. Ideas: *public library, the naturalist at the wildlife reserve.*)

9. (Help students decide which sources will best answer their questions.) Good researchers consult a variety of sources to answer the same question to make sure that their information is as detailed and accurate as possible.

10. (Have students begin their research. Make a variety of resources available to them.) Answer your specific questions on the back of each question card in your own words rather than copying from the source. Write each important point that answers the question on a separate note card. When you use a direct quotation, surround it with quotation marks. Make sure that each source from which you get information is clearly documented on the back of the note card and includes author's first and last names, title (clearly underlined to remind you to type in italics later), city of publication, publishing company, and date of publication.

11. Look at your "research deck" again. Do you need to re-sort the question cards into different groups? Are you satisfied with the groupings that you started with? Do you need to make any changes? Do you need to add new heading cards to your deck?

12. Sort the cards in your "research deck" into a sequence that makes sense. Each group of cards should be set out under its topic heading. Once you are satisfied with the order of your cards, clearly number them.

13. Use the information from your "research deck" to help you write the first draft of your report. Remember to use your own words and to include quotation marks if you have taken a quote from a book.

14. (Have students prepare a draft and a final copy of their reports.)

15. The last part of your report will be a bibliography. A bibliography is a list of the sources that you consulted when you did your research. What is a bibliography? (Signal.) *A list of sources that you consulted when we did our research.* The bibliography goes at the end of your report.

16. (Provide students with a chart or sheet with the following samples of bibliographic entries that follow the style of the American Psychological Association, based on what sources the students used:

Book by one author:

Cherry, L. (1990). *The Great Kapok Tree*. New York: Harcourt Brace Jovanovich, Publishers.

Book with two or more authors:

Wiseman, L. & Smith, M. (1998). *Discovering Ecological Disasters*. San Francisco: Simon and Schuster.

Encyclopedia article:

Rain Forests. (1995). In *World Book Encyclopedia* (Vol. 18, pp. 507–509). Chicago, ILL: World Book Incorporated.

Magazine article:

Martinez, T. (1999, October 21). Saving Our Planet. *Time*, 107, 17–21.

Newspaper article:

Shaw, N. (1997, May 13). Evidence Shows Environmental Destruction. *Victoria Times*, p. 6.

Videotape:

Cameron, Andrew (Producer) & Dodds, Dawn (Director). (1999). *Rachel Carson: A Biography* [Videotape]. Kansas City: State Documentary Film Board.

Web site:

World Wildlife Federation. How You Can Help Save Species. Retrieved March 22, 2001 from the World Wide Web: **http://www.worldwildlife.org**

ADDITIONAL LITERATURE

Following are some additional titles that your students may enjoy during and following this lesson.

Keepers of the Earth by Michael J. Caduto and Joseph Bruchac

Lesson 15

Language Skill Development

Punctuating Split Dialogue

Preparation: Write the following sentences on the chalkboard or on an overhead transparency.

1. **My bike bragged Niki can go faster than yours.**
2. **If you watch closely said Shen you can see it move.**
3. **I hope sighed Ellen that it doesn't rain this weekend.**
4. **Mr. Bianco said Timothy you left your headlights on.**

Time Required: 20 minutes

What do we call the words that people say out loud in a piece of writing? (Signal.) *Dialogue.* What punctuation marks go around the dialogue? (Call on a student. *Quotation marks.*)

Sometimes dialogue is divided into two parts. (Write on the chalkboard: **Run faster Toby suggested or you won't win the race.**) Read this sentence aloud. (Signal.) *Run faster Toby suggested or you won't win the race.*

What is the first part of what Toby says? (Signal.) *Run faster.* When dialogue is split into two parts, you need to put a comma after the first part of what the speaker says. (Put a comma after **faster.**)

What is the second part of what Toby says? (Call on a student. Idea: *Or you won't win the race.*) When the dialogue is split into two parts, you need to introduce the second part of the dialogue with another comma. (Put a comma after suggested.)

Now we're ready to put the quotation marks around the first part of the dialogue. Remember, all the words that a speaker says must be surrounded by quotation marks. Raise your hand if you can tell us where to put the first set of quotation marks. (Call on a student. Idea: *Before* **Run.** Ask a student to put quotation marks before **Run** on the chalkboard.)

Raise your hand if you can tell us where to put the second set of quotation marks. Remember, the second set of quotation marks always goes after the punctuation mark. (Call on a student. Idea: *After the comma.* Ask a student to put quotation marks after the comma on the chalkboard.)

Now we're ready to put in the quotation marks around the second part of the dialogue. What is the second part of what Toby says? (Signal.) *Or you won't win the race.* The second part of the dialogue begins with the word **or,** so the first set of quotation marks is put in front of **or.** (Put quotation marks before **or.**)

Raise your hand if you can tell us where to put the second set of quotation marks. Remember, the second set of quotation marks always goes after the punctuation mark.

(Call on a student. Idea: *After the period.* Ask a student to put quotation marks after the period on the chalkboard.)

(Repeat above process with the following sentence: **Please pass me the lemonade said Luke I am very thirsty.**)

(Point to the sentences on the chalkboard or overhead transparency.) Rewrite each sentence correctly in your notebook using correct punctuation.

Literature

Mini-Novel Study

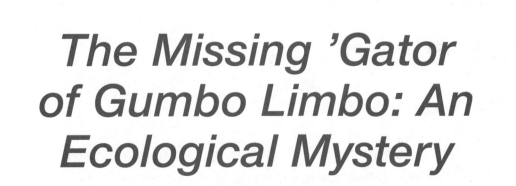

The Missing 'Gator of Gumbo Limbo: An Ecological Mystery

by Jean Craighead George

Materials Required: BLM 15A and 15B, one copy for each student
One copy of the novel for each student

Introducing the Novel

(Hold up a copy of the novel.) Next you will be participating in a novel study.

Read the title of the novel. (Signal.) *The Missing 'Gator of Gumbo Limbo.* Read the subtitle. (Signal.) *An Ecological Mystery.* Read the name of the author. (Signal.) *Jean Craighead George.*

This novel is an ecological mystery. What do you think are the elements of an ecological mystery? (Call on different students. Ideas: *A mystery story about a mysterious ecological event; has clues; a solution.*)

(Give each student a copy of BLM 15A and BLM 15B.) As you read this mystery story, you will complete this analysis sheet. Later you will use the same sheet as a plan for writing your own ecological mystery. (Students may read the novel aloud or silently during class times, in small groups, or with a partner. You may wish to have students work independently through the novels that are found in the remainder of this program. Analysis sheets may be completed as a class activity or individually.)

Answer Key:

3. When: On a warm spangled day
   Where: Florida Everglades

4. The disappearance of the giant alligator, Dajun

5. (Accept reasonable responses.)

6. First person

7. Blue algae in the water; map clues; clear water meant Dajun was in Gumbo Limbo Hole; Parrot said, "night, night"

8. Dajun hid underwater all day, came out at night

9. Development, swamps being drained, pesticides, toxic waste disposal

10. Area was made into a wildlife reserve

11. Lisa K. got a home, James James became caretaker of the reserve

Activity

Writing/Speaking/Listening

Title: *Writing and Revising an Ecological Mystery*
Materials Required: BLM 15A and 15B, another copy for each student

Procedure

1. Now that you have researched ecological issues and read and analyzed an ecological mystery, you are going to use this information to write an ecological mystery of your own. In your story, some strange and mysterious ecological event is going to happen. For example, all the tree frogs in an area will disappear overnight. Write down some ideas and then use your notes to help you think of a mystery you would like to write a story about.

2. (Give each student another copy of BLM 15A and 15B.) You will use these sheets to make a plan that will be the outline for your story. Be sure to include in your story all the elements that are on the sheets.

3. When your plan is ready, write the first draft of your mystery. Ask yourself: Have I included all the information the reader needs to know? Have I included any extra details that distract the reader from my main story line? Are my characters realistic and believable? Ask a friend or relative to read your draft and help you decide what ideas need to be changed or developed further.

4. (Encourage students to use a computer or word processor to write the final copies of their stories. Ensure that students follow the correct formatting conventions for margins, tabs, spacing, columns, and paging.)

5. Read your mystery aloud to a friend, the class, a parent or a relative. Remember to use appropriate rate, volume, and tone. Speak clearly and project your voice. Make eye contact with your audience, and use gestures and expressions to make your speaking more interesting.

ADDITIONAL LITERATURE

Following are some additional titles that your students may enjoy during and following this lesson.

Case of the Missing Cutthroats: An Eco Mystery
by Jean Craighead George

The Fire Bug Connection: An Eco Mystery
by Jean Craighead George

Who Really Killed Cock Robin?: An Eco Mystery
by Jean Craighead George

Ecological Mystery Analysis Sheet

1. Title: _____

2. Author: _____

3. Setting:

   When does the story start? _____

   Where: _____

4. Mysterious Ecological Event: _____

   _____

   _____

5. Character Cluster:

Physical Description ——— Mystery Solver ——— Personality Traits

© SRA/McGraw-Hill. Permission is granted to reproduce this page for classroom use.

6. Point of View: _____

7. Three clues that lead to the solution:

    Clue #1: _____

    Clue #2: _____

    Clue #3: _____

8. Solution: _____

    _____

    _____

9. Environmental factors that are a threat: _____

    _____

    _____

10. How is the habitat or species saved? _____

    _____

    _____

11. Resolution: _____

    _____

© SRA/McGraw-Hill. Permission is granted to reproduce this page for classroom use.

Lesson 16

Language Skill Development

Punctuating Split Dialogue

Time Required: 20 minutes

What are the words that people say out loud in a story called? (Signal.) *Dialogue.* What punctuation marks go around the dialogue? (Signal.) *Quotation marks.*

Sometimes dialogue is divided into two parts. (Write on the chalkboard**: Tell me when dinner is ready said Lydia because I am very hungry.**) Read this sentence aloud. (Signal.) *Tell me when dinner is ready said Lydia because I am very hungry.*

What is the first part of what Lydia says? (Signal.) *Tell me when dinner is ready.* When dialogue is split into two parts, what do you need to put after the first part of what the speaker says? (Signal.) *A comma.* (Put a comma after **ready.**)

What is the second part of what Lydia says? (Signal.) *Because I am very hungry.* What do you need to introduce the second part of the dialogue? (Signal.) A comma. (Put a comma after **Lydia.**)

Now we're ready to put in the quotation marks around the first part of the dialogue. Raise your hand if you can tell us where to put the first set of quotation marks. (Call on a student. Idea: *Before* **Tell.** Ask student to put quotation marks before **tell** on the chalkboard.)

Raise your hand if you can tell us where to put the second set of quotation marks. (Call on a student. Idea: *After the comma.* Ask student to put quotation marks after the comma on the chalkboard.)

Now we're ready to put in the quotation marks around the rest of the dialogue. What is the second part of what Lydia says? (Signal.) *Because I am very hungry.* The second part of the dialogue begins with the word **because,** so the first set of quotation marks is put in front of **because.** (Put quotation marks before **because.**)

Raise your hand if you can tell us where to put the second set of quotation marks. (Call on a student. Idea: *After the period.* Ask student to put quotation marks after the period on the chalkboard.)

(Repeat above process with the following sentence: **Please help me begged the girl I am lost.**)

(Give each student a copy of BLM 16A and 16B.) Correctly punctuate each sentence, using quotation marks around each section of dialogue. Rewrite each sentence correctly on the line provided.

Literature

Mini-Novel Study

The Jazz Man

by Mary Hays Weik

Materials Required: BLMs 16C-16F, one copy for each student,
One copy of the novel for each student

Introducing the Novel

(Hold up a copy of the novel.) Next you will be participating in a novel study.

Read the title of the novel. (Signal.) *The Jazz Man.* Read the name of the author.
(Signal.) *Mary Hays Weik.*

Note: Following discussion of the appropriate chapter word lists, reading for *The Jazz Man* may be done independently, in small groups, or as a whole-group, teacher-directed activity. Word lists and question sets for each chapter are provided. Students may write answers to the questions in their own notebooks.

ADDITIONAL LITERATURE

Following are some additional titles that your students may enjoy during and following this lesson.

Satchmo's Blues by Alan Schroeder

Duke Ellington by Andrea Davis Pinkey

Whitney Houston: Singer, Actress, Superstar by Rosemary Wallner

Answer Key: *The Jazz Man*

Chapter I:

1. (pages 3 and 4) Ideas: Zeke lived in a little dark house. Zeke lived down South and no one missed his family when they were gone. He lived in a small dark house at the edge of a smoky town.

2. (pages 6 and 7) Ideas: Cross, old Mrs. Dowdy had fancy lace curtains on her windows and she made her husband take off his big, muddy shoes at the door. Lispie's room had a crooked green blind and Lispie was mentally handicapped. Old Bill drank from a brown bottle and shouted bad words at you if he caught you looking.

3. (page 6) Zeke had a lame foot and one leg was shorter than the other.

4. (page 6) Ideas: Zeke hid when the school man came. Zeke was afraid other children would make fun of his lameness. Zeke felt different because he was lame.

5. (page10) Zeke thought that a monkey would come out of a door in the side.

6. (page 14) sing, cry, talk, explain

7. Answers will vary.

Chapter II:

1. (page 18) Ideas: The drippy faucet sound like a tiny waterfall in the jungle. The subway sounded like a roaring lion. The windows rattling from the subway sounded like chattering monkeys. The rumble of the city was the wind in the jungle trees.

2. (pages 20, 21, and 22) Ideas: Tony had a laughing red mouth and played the trumpet high and sweet. Manuel got so happy when he played that he flung his drumsticks around.

3. (page 23) Zeke's father couldn't seem to keep a steady job.

4. (page 25) Idea: When she was helping Zeke read, she was crying. The author told us that Zeke kept telling himself she would come home.

5. (page 25) Zeke waited behind the door for a long time because he started to wait when it was getting dark and the streetlights came on before he stopped waiting.

6. Answers will vary.

Chapter III:

1. (pages 26 and 27) No, Zeke's father was not a responsible man because he left Zeke alone for days without food and without anyone to take care of him.

2. Ideas: Zeke became quieter because he didn't want to have to talk to people who came to the door. Zeke got skinnier because he didn't have anything to eat. Zeke's stomach started to ache with hunger. Zeke was shivering because it was cold and he had no food to make him warmer. He was afraid because no one was there to comfort him.

3. (pages 28 and 29) Zeke's neighbors were kind because they brought him food when they could. Zeke's neighbors were cruel because they knew Zeke didn't have a rich Auntie to help him and they knew Zeke's mother was not coming back.

4. Idea: The author made the Jazz Man go away because he brought happiness to Zeke. There isn't supposed to be any happiness in this chapter.

Chapter IV:

1. (page 36) After a million years, he reached the street.

2. Idea: Zeke was very ill because he was so hungry and cold.

3. Idea: I thought Zeke was going to look for his mother/father/the Jazz Man.

4. Answers will vary widely. Look for the descriptive details to be reflected in the drawings.

5. Answers will vary.

Proofread each sentence. Rewrite each sentence correctly on the line provided.

1. Please pass me your plate said Kim but only if you've finished eating.

_____

2. Don't eat me warned the mouse or you will get a stomachache.

_____

3. If you look over that hill said Shalen you can see my house.

_____

4. When you find your baseball said Gavin we can play catch.

_____

5. You may have a cookie now she promised if you eat all your broccoli later.

_____

© SRA/McGraw-Hill. Permission is granted to reproduce this page for classroom use.

Proofread each sentence. Rewrite each sentence correctly on the line provided.

1. In your opinion inquired Jennifer do you think I should wear my red blouse

_____

2. What can I say asked Donna to make you change your mind

_____

3. Look out yelled Chris that branch is going to fall

_____

4. On your way home she asked could you pick up some milk

_____

5. If I have to write any longer groaned Juan my hand will fall off

_____

© SRA/McGraw-Hill. Permission is granted to reproduce this page for classroom use.

The Jazz Man: Word List, Chapter I

I	II	III
topmost	squinting	mite
brownstone	business	carriage
downstairs	groceries	mysterious
anybody	practise	disappeared

The Jazz Man: Questions, Chapter I

Use a full sentence to answer each question.

1. Where did Zeke live before he moved to the topmost floor of the brownstone?

2. Tell what you know about two of Zeke's neighbors.

3. Why did Zeke's Mama say that Zeke walked with a "cute little hop step"?

4. Why do you think Zeke didn't go to school?

5. When Zeke saw the big brown box, what did he think would happen?

6. On page 14, the author uses words to describe the music the Jazz Man made. Those words make the music seem like a person. Write those four words on your page.

7. The Jazz Man's music made Zeke feel happy. Tell about music that makes you feel happy. Write a paragraph of at least five sentences.

© SRA/McGraw-Hill. Permission is granted to reproduce this page for classroom use.

The Jazz Man: Word List, Chapter II

I	II	III
wonderful	no-job blues	jigetty
happiness	universe	drippy
trumpet	Puerto Rican	African
saxophone	tavern	session

The Jazz Man: Questions, Chapter II

Use a full sentence to answer each question.

1. After the Jazz Man came, Zeke felt like he was living in a wonderful new world. Tell in three or four sentences how Zeke's world had changed (page 18).

2. Tell what you know about two of the Jazz Man's musician friends.

3. Tell about the problem with Zeke's father.

4. How did you know that Zeke's mother was not coming home even before the author told you?

5. Did Zeke wait behind the door for a long time? How do you know?

6. How will Zeke's life change now that his mother is gone? Answer in a paragraph of at least five sentences.

© SRA/McGraw-Hill. Permission is granted to reproduce this page for classroom use.

I	II	III
quieter skinnier ache shivering afraid	landlord toothpicks sideways	scaredy-cats seldom embarrass apt tales wrinkled

The Jazz Man: **Questions, Chapter III**

Use a full sentence to answer each question.

1. Was Zeke's father a responsible man? Tell how you know.

2. The words in column 1 of your word list describe Zeke and what happened to him. Choose three of the words and use them in sentences to tell what was happening to Zeke.

3. Zeke's neighbors were kind and cruel. Tell how they were kind. Tell how they were cruel.

4. The author made the Jazz Man go away during this chapter. Why would she do that?

The Jazz Man: **Word List, Chapter III**

© SRA/McGraw-Hill. Permission is granted to reproduce this page for classroom use.

The Jazz Man: **Word List, Chapter IV**

I	II	III
pitchy-dark stairrail mixed-up	drizzle inviting hazy elephant scrooched	slippery green glittery

The Jazz Man: **Questions, Chapter IV**
Use a full sentence to answer each question.

1. It took a long time for Zeke to get down the stairs. Copy the sentence that tells you that it took a long time.

2. Tell what you thought was wrong with Zeke when you read pages 35 and 36.

3. When you read page 37, whom did you think Zeke was going to look for?

4. Read the paragraph that begins on the bottom of page 36 and ends on line 7 of page 37. Draw a color picture of what you have read.

5. Were you surprised by the ending of this story? Tell why or why not in a paragraph of four or five sentences.

© SRA/McGraw-Hill. Permission is granted to reproduce this page for classroom use.

Lesson 17

Language Skill Development

Punctuating Split Dialogue

Time Required: 20 minutes

What are the words that people say out loud in a story called? (Signal.) *Dialogue.* What punctuation marks go around the dialogue? (Signal.) *Quotation marks.*

Sometimes dialogue is divided into two parts. (Write on the chalkboard: **Too much sun warned Dr. Morrison may be harmful.**) Read this sentence aloud. (Signal.) *Too much sun warned Dr. Morrison may be harmful.*

What is the first part of what Dr. Morrison says? (Signal.) *Too much sun.* When dialogue is split into two parts, what punctuation mark do you need to put after the first part of what the speaker says? (Signal.) *A comma.* (Put a comma after **sun.**)

What is the second part of what Dr. Morrison says? (Call on a student. Idea: *May be harmful.*) When the dialogue is split into two parts, what punctuation mark do you need to introduce the second part of the dialogue? (Signal.) *A comma.* (Put a comma after **Morrison.**)

Now we're ready to put in the quotation marks around the first part of the dialogue. Raise your hand if you can tell us where to put the first set of quotation marks. (Call on a student. Idea: *Before* **Too.** Ask student to put quotation marks before **Too** on the chalkboard.)

Raise your hand if you can tell us where to put the second set of quotation marks. (Call on a student. Idea: *After the comma.* Ask student to put quotation marks after the comma on the chalkboard.)

Now we're ready to put the quotation marks around the second part of the dialogue. What is the second part of what Dr. Morrison says? (Signal.) *May be harmful.* Where do we put the next set of quotation marks? (Call on a student. Idea: *Before the word* **May.** Ask student to put quotation marks before **May** on the chalkboard.)

Raise your hand if you can tell us where to put the last set of quotation marks. (Call on a student. Idea: *After the period.* Ask student to put quotation marks after the period on the chalkboard.)

(Repeat above process with the following sentence: Hercules commented the professor was a mythical Greek hero.)

(Give each student a copy of BLM 17A.) Correctly punctuate each sentence, using quotation marks around each section of dialogue. Rewrite each sentence correctly on the line provided.

Literature

The Most Beautiful Place in the World

by Ann Cameron

Materials Required: BLM 17A and BLM 17B, one copy for each student
One copy of the novel for each student

Introducing the Novel

(Hold up a copy of the novel.) Next you will be participating in a novel study.

Read the title of the novel. (Signal.) *The Most Beautiful Place in the World.* Read the name of the author. (Signal.) *Ann Cameron.*

> **Note:** Following discussion of the appropriate chapter word lists, reading for *The Most Beautiful Place in the World* may be done independently, in small groups, or as a whole-group, teacher-directed activity. Word lists and question sets for each part are provided. Students may write answers to the questions in their own notebooks.

The Most Beautiful Place in the World: Answer Key, Part 1

1. Idea: There should be three volcanoes, a lake, eight villages, a road and perhaps, a ferryboat. Other details may be included if justifiable.

2. Ideas: A man wearing a white hat is carrying a number of brooms on his shoulder. A man with a walking stick is leading a mule that is carrying firewood. A woman is carrying a basket on her head. There are two dogs and a bus in the picture.

3. (page 21) *Arroz con leche* means rice with milk. It is like rice pudding that you drink instead of eat. It is sweet and it has cinnamon in it.

4. Ideas: San Pablo is not a modern town because there aren't many cars. Juan's grandmother's house doesn't have hot water in the shower or electricity. You have to carry most things because there aren't many cars.

The Most Beautiful Place in the World: Answer Key, Part 2

5. (page 25) Juan's mother took the bed when Juan's grandmother wasn't home. She may not have let her take it if she had been home.

6. Answers will vary. All should begin with "I resemble my _____ because..."

7. (page 29) The rule is that you must be back inside before 8:30. After that, you will not be let in by Grandmother or anyone else.

8. Answers will vary.

The Most Beautiful Place in the World: Answer Key, Part 3

1. (page 37) Juan wanted to punch his stepbrother because he was jealous. He didn't do it because he knew that what happened to him wasn't the kid's fault.

2. (page 40) Juan's grandmother helped him to become a good worker by teaching him how to ladle the *arroz con leche* and to make change. Then she taught him to shine shoes perfectly every time.

3. (page 41) Juan started to make about one dollar every day. It doesn't seem like very much money to me.

4. (page 43) Juan was afraid to ask because he thought that Grandmother liked him only because he made money for her.

5. (page 46) She didn't know that Juan had turned seven.

The Most Beautiful Place in the World: Answer Key, Part 4

6. Answers will vary

7. (page 51) Juan's Aunt Tina had never thought much of Juan. She was surprised that he was doing so well in school. (refer to page 57)

8. Answers will vary.

The Most Beautiful Place in the World: Word List, Part 1, pages 13 — 24 (finish at line 14)

I	II	III
Guatemala San Pablo volcanoes hummingbirds arroz con leche	language thousands vegetables balanced naturally	stroll conversation especially caretaker fought

The Most Beautiful Place in the World: Questions, Part 1

Use a full sentence to answer each question.

1. Draw and label a map of San Pablo using the information on pages 13 and 14.
2. Look carefully at the picture of San Pablo on pages 16 and 17. Write three sentences describing what you see.
3. Describe *arroz con leche* as though you were telling a friend about it. Write two or three sentences.
4. Would you say that San Pablo is a modern town? Why or why not?

The Most Beautiful Place in the World: Word List, Part 2, pages 24 — 35 (start at line 8 and finish at line 3)

I	II
resembles bought stepfather worried understood	shivering shiver bananas creaked

The Most Beautiful Place in the World: Questions, Part 2

Use a full sentence to answer each question.

5. Read page 26 again. Do you think that Juan's mother stole the bed? Why or why not?
6. On page 24 we learn that Juan resembles his mother. Whom do you resemble? Describe how you resemble that person. Begin your answer with "I resemble (my mother, my father, or someone else) because…"
7. Tell about the gate rule at Grandmother's house.
8. Is the gate rule fair or unfair? Tell why or why not.

© SRA/McGraw-Hill. Permission is granted to reproduce this page for classroom use.

**The Most Beautiful Place in the World: Word List, Part 3, pages 35 — 47
(start at line 3 and finish to the end of page 47)**

I	II	III
unbolted tiptoed whispered borrowed realized	accident somersaults backflips ladle	customers tourist office newspaper important

The Most Beautiful Place in the World: Questions, Part 3

Use a full sentence to answer each question.

1. Tell about Juan's feelings for his baby stepbrother.

2. How did Juan's grandmother help him to become a good worker (page 40)?

3. How much money did Juan make when he became good at shining shoes? Does it seem like much money to you?

4. Why was Juan afraid to ask his grandmother about going to school (page 43)?

5. Why hadn't Juan's grandmother sent him to school before now (page 46)?

The Most Beautiful Place in the World: Word List, Part 4, pages 48 — 57

I	II	III
first-grade politely arithmetic admitted permission	enough tragedy congratulations enroll	complain university figure special inconvenient

The Most Beautiful Place in the World: Questions, Part 4

Use a full sentence to answer each question.

6. Grandmother got Juan into school because she was persistent — she didn't give up. Tell about something you have done where not giving up was important. Write a paragraph of five or six sentences.

7. Why was Juan's Aunt Tina so surprised (page 51) when she read Juan's note?

8. Grandmother thinks that the most beautiful place in the world is anyplace you can be proud of being yourself. Juan thinks the most beautiful place in the world is anyplace where you love someone a lot and you know that they love you. What do you think the most beautiful place in the world is? Why? Explain in four or five complete sentences.

© SRA/McGraw-Hill. Permission is granted to reproduce this page for classroom use.

Lesson 18

Language Skill Development
Capitalizing Nationalities and Historical Events

Time Required: 20 minutes

Preparation: Write the following paragraph on the chalkboard or an overhead transparency:

Dora wanted to learn swahili, but ashbury junior high school offered only spanish classes. dora had been to egypt and new zealand, but never spain. her father had been overseas during the vietnam war. Her grandfather had served in hawaii during world war II. dora's mother had traveled to england to study the middle ages. last june, her family hosted a nigerian student who spoke french, hausa, english, and hebrew.

Raise your hand if you can tell us an example of a kind of word that is capitalized in sentences. (Call on different students. Record answers on the chalkboard for students to refer to. Ideas: *I; people's names; names of towns; names of streets; names of public buildings; states; countries; the first word in a sentence.*)

The names of races, nationalities, and languages should be capitalized. (Write on the chalkboard: **Native American, German, Spanish, African American, Italian, Australian.**) Read this list of races, nationalities, and languages aloud. (Signal.) *Native American, German, Spanish, African American, Italian, Australian.* Raise your hand if you can think of any other nationalities that should be capitalized. (Call on different students. Accept correct responses.)

The names of historical events and periods also should be capitalized. (Write on the chalkboard: **World War II, the Vietnam War, the Boston Tea Party, the Middle Ages, the Great Depression.**) Read this list of historical events and periods aloud. (Signal.) *World War II, the Vietnam War, the Boston Tea Party, the Middle Ages, the Great Depression.*) Raise your hand if you can think of any other historical events or periods that should be capitalized. (Call on different students. Accept correct responses.)

(Point to the paragraph on the chalkboard.) This paragraph has many errors. Words that should have capitals have none, and words that shouldn't be capitalized have capitals. Read the paragraph. (Call on different students to read parts of the paragraph aloud or have students read the paragraph silently.)

We are going to proofread this paragraph. Read the first sentence. (Signal.) *Dora wanted to learn swahili, but ashbury junior high school only offered spanish classes.* Raise your hand if you can tell us where a capitalization mistake needs to be corrected in the first sentence. (Call on a student. Idea: **Swahili** needs a capital because it is a language.) I will put three little lines under the **s** to remind me to capitalize **swahili**. What proofreading mark do I write to show that a word should be capitalized? (Signal.) *Three little lines.*

Raise your hand if you can tell us where another capitalization mistake needs to be corrected in the first sentence. (Call on a student. Idea: *Ashbury junior high school should be capitalized because it is the name of an institution.*) I will put three little lines under the **a,** the **j,** the **h,** and the **s** to remind me to capitalize **ashbury junior high school.** What proofreading mark do I write to show that a word should be capitalized? (Signal.) *Three little lines.*

Raise your hand if you can tell us where another capitalization mistake needs to be corrected in the first sentence. (Call on a student. Idea: *Spanish should be capitalized because it's a language.*) I will put three little lines under the **s** to remind me to capitalize **spanish.** What proofreading mark do I write to show that a word needs a capital letter? (Signal.) *Three little lines.* (Repeat process until all errors are corrected.)

(Have students copy the paragraph with corrections into their notebooks for further reinforcement of this skill.)

When you are writing stories and paragraphs of your own, remember to proofread your writing for the correct use of capital letters.

Literature

Materials Required: BLM 18A and 18B, one copy for each student
One copy of the novel for each student

Run Away Home
by Patricia C. McKissack

Introducing the Novel

(Hold up a copy of the novel.) Next you will be participating in a novel study.

Read the title of the novel. (Signal.) *Run Away Home.* Read the name of the author. (Signal.) *Patricia C. McKissack.*

This novel is historical fiction. When a novel is based on facts from a true story that really happened in the past, it is called historical fiction. What is it called when a novel is based on facts from a true story that really happened in the past? (Signal.) *Historical fiction.* When we read historical fiction, we learn about how people lived a long time ago. What do we learn when we read historical fiction? (Signal.) *How people lived a long time ago.*

Open your novels to the author's note found on Roman numeral page seven. The author has provided you with historical background knowledge about the time period in which this novel was written.

(Give each student a copy of BLM 18A.) You will read the Author's Note and take notes on this sheet about the historical time period in which this novel is set. Cues have been provided on the sheet to help you decide what information is important.

(After students have completed the note-taking exercise, check notes for correct information. Discuss the information further with the students and ask them if they know any other information about this time period in history, about sharecropping, and about the Apache. Students may complete further research in print materials or by using electronic media.)

(Following the discussion, reading for *The Most Beautiful Place in the World* may be done independently, in small groups, or as a whole-group, teacher-directed activity.

ADDITIONAL LITERATURE

Following are some additional titles that your students may enjoy during and following this lesson.

Aunt Harriet's Underground Railroad in the Sky by Faith Ringgold

A Picture of Freedom: The Diary of Clotee, a Slave Girl, Belmont Plantation, 1859 by Patricia C. McKissack

Tennessee Trailblazers by Patricia C. McKissack

Answer Key for Exercise #1   *Run Away Home*
Author's Note

I. Geronimo, 39 Apache, U.S. Army

    A) Florida, two years

        1. Southwest   2. sent to Florida

    B) Alabama, Oklahoma

II. A) Full citizens with equal protection under U.S. Constitution

    B) Withdrawn from South

        1. "Jim Crow"   (a) blacks, whites

    C) Jobs, education

        1. Slavery

        2. North or West

    D) Stop blacks from voting

        1. If a person was qualified to vote

        (a) How many bubbles in a bar of soap?

        (b) How high is up?

        (c) memorize the whole constitution

        2. Right to vote

    E) intimidated, illegal

        1. Schools, businesses

        2. Property

        3. People

           a) Seventy   b) Sixty-nine lynched

I. In 1886, _____ and _____ surrendered to

_____.

   A. sent to _____ for _____

      1. then could return to _____

      2. other Apache also _____

   B. May 1888 moved to _____ and in 1894 to _____

II. 1880s difficult years for blacks.

   A. Civil War made them _____

   B. 1877 federal troops were _____

   C. _____ and _____ were limited.

   D. Laws were passed to _____

      1. literacy tests to determine _____

         a) _____?

         b) _____?

         c) _____

      2. caused blacks to lose _____

   E. Violent white supremacy groups _____ blacks even though

they were _____.

      1. burned _____ and _____

      2. destroyed _____

      3. murdered _____

         a) 1887 _____

         b) 1888 _____

© SRA/McGraw-Hill. Permission is granted to reproduce this page for classroom use.

Writing Activity

Using the information you learned from doing BLM 18A and the knowledge you gained from reading *Run Away Home*, write a short report about how you think minority groups were treated in the post (after) Civil War period.

© SRA/McGraw-Hill. Permission is granted to reproduce this page for classroom use.

Lesson 19

Language Skill Development
Capitalizing Places and Geographical Features

Time required: 30 minutes

Preparation: Write the following paragraph on the chalkboard or an overhead transparency:

> mrs. Motesa and her son mark just returned from a vacation in africa. mark liked the sahara desert, But mrs. motesa preferred the tropical forests of cameroon better. They spent a week in zimbabwe, then traveled to uganda, congo,and gabon. in June they stayed near lake tanganyika, Then they went up to lake victoria, which connects to the nile river far North near the red sea. it was a beautiful trip.

Raise your hand if you can tell us an example of a kind of word that is capitalized in sentences. (Call on several students. Accept all correct responses. Record answers on the chalkboard for students to refer to. Ideas: *I; people's names; names of towns; names of streets; names of public buildings; states; countries; the first word in a sentence.*)

The names of lakes, rivers, oceans, mountains, and other natural and man-made landmarks all should be capitalized. (Write on the chalkboard: **the Atlantic Ocean, Red Sea, Mount Everest, Lake Tahoe, the Grand Canyon, the Eiffel Tower.**) Read the list aloud. (Signal.) *The Atlantic Ocean, Mount Everest, Lake Tahoe, the Grand Canyon, the Eiffel Tower.* Raise your hand if you can think of any other oceans, mountains, lakes, or man-made monuments that need to be capitalized. (Call on different students. Accept correct responses.)

(Point to the paragraph on the chalkboard.) This paragraph has many errors. Words that should have capitals have none and words that shouldn't be capitalized have capitals. Read the paragraph. (Call on different students to read parts of the paragraph aloud or have students read the paragraph silently.)

We are going to proofread this paragraph. Read the first sentence. (Signal.) *Mrs. Motesa and her son Mark just returned from a vacation in Africa.* Raise your hand if you can tell us where a capitalization mistake needs to be corrected in the first sentence. (Call on a student. Idea: *Mrs. motesa should be capitalized because it is a proper name.*) I will put three little lines under the **m** in **mrs.** and the **m** in **motesa** to remind me to capitalize Mrs. Motesa's name. What proofreading mark do I write to show that a word needs to be capitalized? (Signal.) *Three little lines.* (Repeat process until all errors are corrected.)

(Have students copy the paragraph with corrections into their notebooks for further reinforcement of this skill.)

When you are writing stories and paragraphs of your own, remember to proofread your writing for the correct use of capital letters.

Literature

Materials Required: BLM 19A, B, and C, one copy for each student
One copy of the novel for each student

Number the Stars

by Lois Lowry

Introducing the Novel

(Hold up a copy of the novel.) Next you will be participating in a novel study.

Read the title of the novel. (Signal.) *Number the Stars.* Read the name of the author. (Signal.) *Lois Lowry.*

This novel is historical fiction. What is historical fiction? (Call on a student. Idea: *A story that is based on facts from a true story that really happened in the past*.) What do we learn when we read historical fiction? (Signal.) *How people lived a long time ago.*

(Give each student a copy of BLM 19A.) This is an information passage. It tells you important background information about the historical time period in which this novel is set.

Now let's read and discuss the passage. (Call on different students to read a portion of the passage aloud. Discuss the main ideas of the passage.)

You are going to make an outline from what you read in this passage. An **outline** is a plan that helps you organize information about what you read. What's an outline? (Signal.) *A plan that helps you organize information about what you read.*

Reread the information passage and then make an outline. When we make outlines we use Roman numerals to show the most important heading. When do we use Roman numerals? (Signal.) *When we want to show the most important heading.* We use capital letters, lowercase letters, and numbers to show the details about the most important heading.

Fill in the outline. (After students have completed the outlining exercise, check outlines for correct information. Discuss the information further with the students and ask them if they know any other information about this time period in history. Students may complete further research in print materials or by using electronic media.)

(Following the discussion, reading for *Number the Stars* may be done independently, in small groups, or as a whole-group, teacher-directed activity.

ADDITIONAL LITERATURE

Following are some additional titles that your students may enjoy during and following this lesson.

Lily's Crossing by Patricia Reilly Giff

High Flight: A Story of World War II by Linda Granfield

From Anna by Jean Little

Answer Key for Exercise #1   Outlining

I. Adolph Hitler
  A. leader of Germany, 1933
  B. corporal, German army
  C. he helped form the

II. NAZISM
  A. were superior and should rule the world
  B. to expand its borders and get more land
  C. should be removed from German society
    1. (a) against Jews   (b) exterminated

III. World War II
  A. Poland, Denmark, Norway, Holland, Belgium, and France
    (a) part of army in countries
    (b) supported Germans
    (c) resisted German occupation
       i) blow up train tracks
       ii) bomb factories
       iii) kill German soldiers
    (d) relocated
       i) concentration, slave labor
       ii) extermination, exterminated
       iii) six, Jews were killed, Holocaust

Exercise # 1   Background passage and note-taking sheet

Adolph Hitler was elected leader of Germany in 1933. Fifteen years earlier he was not a famous person. He had been a corporal in the German army in World War I (1914–1918), and then after the war, he helped form a new political party. The new political party was called the Nazi Party. It had as its symbol a swastika. Hitler was the main spokesman for this party and he outlined its philosophies.

Nazism stood for many ideas. One idea was that people from Northern Europe (Nordic People) were Aryans and that they were superior to all other people on Earth and they should rule the world. Another idea was that Germany needed to expand its borders and take more land from other "inferior" races of people. A third idea was that people who were not what Nazis called "true Germans" should be removed from German society. The Nazis were Anti-Semites, which meant that they were against Jews. The Nazis believed that all Jews should be exterminated.

In 1939 Hitler started World War II by invading Poland. In the next year he took over Holland, Belgium, Denmark, Norway, and France. He had built up a very strong army, and these countries were unprepared for war. In 1941 he invaded the Soviet Union with the idea of getting more "living space" for Germany.

When Germany took over a country, they had to "occupy" it. This meant keeping part of the army in that country to control it. In every country there were some sympathizers. These were people who, for the most part, supported what the Nazis stood for. In most countries there were also resistance fighters. These were individuals and groups who resisted German occupation. They would do things to try to stop the German war effort, like blowing up train tracks, stopping trains from moving, and bombing factories that were making military equipment and supplies for Germany. They would even sometimes kill German soldiers.

In the occupied lands, Jews were rounded up and relocated. This meant that they were sent to special camps where they were to be used as slaves—working for the war effort. These camps were called **concentration camps** and were set up in Germany and in some occupied countries. Jews and other "undesirables" who were not healthy enough to work were exterminated. During World War II (1939–1945), about 6,000,000 Jews and others were murdered by the Nazis. This slaughter of Jews is called the Holocaust.

© SRA/McGraw-Hill. Permission is granted to reproduce this page for classroom use.

Outline for Exercise #1

I Adolph Hitler

    A. elected _____ in _____.

    B. had been a _____ in _____ in World War I.

    C. after war _____ Nazi Party.

II NAZISM

    A. Aryans _____.

    B. Germany needed _____.

    C. Undesirables _____.

        1. Anti-Semitic:

           (a) _____

           (b) Jews should be _____

III World War II

    A. Hitler took over _____

    _____.

        1. Occupied them:

           (a) keeping _____.

           (b) sympathizers _____.

           (c) resistance fighters _____.

               i) _____.

               ii) _____.

               iii) _____.

© SRA/McGraw-Hill. Permission is granted to reproduce this page for classroom use.

(d) Jews rounded up and _____.

    i) _____ camps for _____.

    ii) _____ camps to be _____.

    iii) _____ million _____ during the

part of the war called the _____.

Exercise #2

Using as many terms as you can from Exercise #1 and knowledge gained from reading *Number the Stars*, describe Nazi Germany's program for getting rid of Jewish people.

© SRA/McGraw-Hill. Permission is granted to reproduce this page for classroom use.

This passage has many errors. Words that should have capitals have none, and words that shouldn't be capitalized have capitals. First read the paragraph silently to yourself. Next correct capitalization mistakes using the correct proofreading mark. Finally copy the paragraph correctly.

Many countries are known for their landmarks. In egypt, the great pyramid of giza is very famous, as is the statue of liberty at the entrance of the harbor in new york city. the leaning tower of pisa in italy and the eiffel tower in paris are also very well known. tourists flock to greece to visit the parthenon and the temple of Athena. If you visit san Francisco, be sure to see the golden gate bridge.

Natural landmarks may be even more striking. The grand canyon, for example, in arizona's grand canyon national park, has incredible views. The nile river has made egypt famous, just like mount everest made nepal a popular destination for mountain climbers. a massive orange rock in central australia called uluru, or sometimes called ayers rock, is instantly recognizable.

A book titled natural wonders of the world will help you find more information about these Great Monuments. You can find it in the springfield municipal library, Which is located at the corner of osborne street and denby lane, near kensington memorial park. The head librarian, mr. anansi, will help you find it.

_____

_____

_____

_____

_____

_____

_____

_____

_____

_____

© SRA/McGraw-Hill. Permission is granted to reproduce this page for classroom use.

Lesson 20

Language Skill Development

Capitalization of Titles and Names of Relatives

Time Required: 30 minutes

Preparation: Write the following paragraph on the chalkboard or an overhead transparency:

candace and janice wanted to see a Movie at the cityplex six Theater. the movie they hoped to see was Titled night of darkness. candace said goodbye to her Grandma and left to meet Juanita on the corner of Birch street and princess avenue. together they walked down pitney boulevard to hillside mall, where the Movie Theatre was located. juanita stopped at party snacks treat Shop to buy jellybeans. mrs. Yotimo, Who worked in the Ticket Booth, said night of darkness was sold out, but they could see danger beach instead. candace said father saw it and thought it was good.

Raise your hand if you can tell us an example of a kind of word that is capitalized in sentences. (Call on several students. Accept all correct responses. Record answers on the chalkboard for students to refer to. Ideas: *People's names; names of streets and highways; public recreation centers; names of parks; countries; shops; shopping malls; banks*.)

Names of parents and relatives need to be capitalized only if they are being used in place of a person's proper name. (Write on the chalkboard: **On Saturday, Mother said I could wear this dress.**) Read this sentence aloud. (Signal.) *On Saturday, Mother said I could wear this dress.*

In this sentence, the name Mother could be replaced by a proper name. Let's substitute the name **Carol** for **Mother** and read the sentence again. (Signal.) *On Saturday, Carol said I could wear this dress.* Does the sentence make sense? (Signal.) *Yes.* If you can substitute a proper name for the name of a parent or relative, then that parent or relative's name needs to be capitalized.

(Write on the chalkboard: **Please ask your grandfather if he would like some lemonade.**) Read this sentence aloud. (Signal.) *Please ask your grandfather if he would like some lemonade.* Let's substitute the proper name **Henry** for **grandfather** and read the sentence again. (Signal.) *Please ask your Henry if he would like some lemonade.* Does the sentence make sense? (Signal.) *No.* If you can't substitute a proper name for the name of a parent or relative, then that parent or relative's name should not be capitalized.

Titles of movies and books need to be capitalized. (Write on the chalkboard: **The Mystery of Black Hill.**) Read the title of this book aloud. (Signal.) *The Mystery of Black Hill.* The first word of a title is always capitalized. What is the first word of this title? (Signal.) *The.* Is it capitalized? (Signal.) *Yes.* All the important words in the rest of the title need to be capitalized as well. What are the important words in this book title?

(Call on a student. Ideas: *Mystery, Black, hill.*) Little words like **and, by**, and **of** do not need to be capitalized. Is the word **of** in this title capitalized? (Signal.) *No.*

(Point to the paragraph on the chalkboard.) This paragraph has many errors. Words that should have capitals have none and words that shouldn't be capitalized have capitals. Read the paragraph. (Call on different students to read parts of the paragraph aloud or have students read the paragraph silently.)

We are going to proofread this paragraph. Read the first sentence. (Signal.) *Candace and Juanita wanted to see a movie at the cityplex six theater.* Raise your hand if you can tell us where a capitalization mistake should be corrected in the first sentence. (Call on a student. Idea: *Candace needs a capital because it is a proper name.*) I will put three little lines under the **c** to remind me to put a capital on the name **Candace.**

Raise your hand if you can tell us where another capitalization mistake needs to be proofread in the first sentence. (Call on a student. Idea: *Movie does not need a capital letter.*) I will draw a line through the **M** to remind me to put a lowercase m on movie. What proofreading mark do I write to show that a word should be capitalized? (Signal.) *Three little lines.* What proofreading mark do I write to show that a word should not be capitalized? (Signal.) *Draw a line through the letter that does not need a capital letter.* (Repeat process until all errors are corrected.)

(Have students copy the paragraph with corrections into their notebooks for further reinforcement of this skill.)

When you are writing stories and paragraphs of your own, remember to proofread your writing for the correct use of capital letters.

Literature

Materials Required: BLM 20A and 20B, one copy for each student
One copy of the novel for each student

Red Scarf Girl

by Ji-Li Jiang

Introducing the Novel

(Hold up a copy of the novel.) Next you will be participating in a novel study.

Read the title of the novel. (Signal.) *Red Scarf Girl.* Read the name of the author. (Signal.) *Ji-Li Jiang.*

This novel is historical fiction. What is it called when a novel is based on facts from a true story that really happened in the past? (Signal.) *Historical fiction.* What do we learn when we read historical fiction? (Signal.) *How people lived a long time ago.*

This novel took place during the Cultural Revolution in China. It was a very difficult time for many people who lived in China. As you read the novel, try to get a picture in your mind of what it would have been like to be a teenager during that time. This book is written from the first person point of view. It is the main character, Ji-Li Jiang, who tells the story. It is her personal narrative about her life during this time period.

(Following the discussion, reading for *Red Scarf Girl* may be done independently, in small groups, or as a whole-group, teacher-directed activity. Have students complete Exercise #1 as they read the novel. Exercises #2 and #3 are to be completed after students have read the novel. The goal of the exercises is for students to realize that different sources will give them different information ranging from the generalities of events mentioned in the story to the specifics of definitions from a glossary. Exercise #4 gives students the opportunity to synthesize and express the information that they learned the first three exercises.

ADDITIONAL LITERATURE

Following are some additional titles that your students may enjoy during and following this lesson.

Dragonwings by Laurence Yep

American Dragons: Twenty-Five Asian American Voices by Laurence Yep

Answer Key for Exercise #1   The Cultural Revolution

1. beloved leader of China
2. old ideas, old culture, old customs, and old habits
3. keep China from losing her Communist ideals
4. When Red Guards or Neighborhood Dictatorship Groups would enter people's homes in search of counterrevolutionaries or "blacks."
5. a) was called a Black Whelp and excluded from being a Red Successor
   b) arrested and lost his job as an actor
   c) Punished for having been married to a landlord. Had to sweep the streets every day.

Answer Key for Exercise #2   The Cultural Revolution

1. A. Chairman of the Chinese Communist Party
    B. leader of China from 1949 to 1976
2. symbolized opponents of communism
    A. symbolic color of communism
    B. Five Black Catagories
        1. landlords
        2. rich peasants
        3. counterrevolutionaries
        4. criminals
        5. rightists
    C. child of a family of one of the five Black Categories
3. A. classifying people by their economic situation or occupation
        1. One was a revolutionary
        2. One was unreliable
4. A. upheaval that overtook China from 1966–76
        1. people persecuted
        2. Chairman Mao
        3. his own political position
5. A. groups that monitored the activities of neighbors
6. high school, college
        1. loyal supporters and the pioneers of the Cultural
7. Red Guards, elementary
8. A. intended to promote a particular belief

Exercise #1   The Cultural Revolution in China

What was the Cultural Revolution from Ji-Li's point of view? From just reading the story, identify or explain each of the following:

1. Mao Ze-dong (chapter 1) _____

_____

_____

2. The four olds (chapter 2) _____

_____

_____

The objectives of destroying the four olds (p. 28–29) _____

_____

_____

3. House searches _____

_____

4. Describe the ill treatment of

    (a) Ji-Li _____

    _____

    (b) Her father _____

    _____

    (c) Her grandmother _____

    _____

© SRA/McGraw-Hill. Permission is granted to reproduce this page for classroom use.

Exercise #2   The Cultural Revolution in China

Using the glossary on pages 273 to 285, write explanatory definitions for the following items:

1. Mao Ze-dong

   A. _____

   B. _____

2. Black: _____

   A. Red _____
   B. Five Black categories:

      1. _____

      2. _____

      3. _____

      4. _____

      5. _____
   C. Black whelp

      A. _____

3. Class Status

      1. _____

      2. _____

4. Cultural Revolution: Official title _____

   A. _____

      1. _____

      2. _____

      3. _____

5. Neighborhood Dictatorship Groups

   A. _____

© SRA/McGraw-Hill. Permission is granted to reproduce this page for classroom use.

6. Red Guards: very popular organization of _____ and

_____ students.

   A. Chairman Mao's _____

   _____ Revolution.

7. Red Successors

   A. Initiative of _____ in _____ schools.

8. Propaganda

   A. _____

Exercise #3   The Cultural Revolution in China

Using dictionaries, encyclopedias, or other sources, look up the following terms and write a definition for these terms:

1. Capitalism: _____

2. Communism: _____

3. Revolutionary: _____

4. Counterrevolutionary: _____

5. Dictatorship: _____

6. Democracy: _____

7. Conservative: _____

8. Revisionist: _____

9. Leftist: _____

10. Rightist: _____

11. Propaganda: _____

Exercise #4   The Cultural Revolution in China

Using terms from exercises #2 and #3 and knowledge gained from reading *Red Scarf Girl,* tell the story of the Cultural Revolution in China.

© SRA/McGraw-Hill. Permission is granted to reproduce this page for classroom use.

This paragraph has many errors. Words that should have capitals have none and words that shouldn't be capitalized have capitals. Dialogue is missing quotation marks and correct punctuation. First read the paragraph silently to yourself. Next correct capitalization and dialogue mistakes. Finally copy the paragraph correctly.

russel, Jin, and clint are going fishing on saturday. jin said we should buy bait at sherman's fish and tackle shop on king street. Russel said what a great idea! they both walked down church street to the Shop friday after School was out. Mrs. Warner said The best bait to use is a type of worm called red wrigglers. then she showed them a book titled burt's guide to fishing in north america. it had pictures of different kinds of fish from mexico to up to washington. That is the fish I want to catch said Jin. ha ha laughed Russel that fish weighs more than you do!
saturday morning, clint asked his Father if he could borrow grandpa's old fishing rod. sure you can replied Clint's father but make sure that you don't lose it. russel knew that the best place to fish was in hood river near elliott lake. jin's Father drove the boys down highway fourteen to dawsonville, then turned onto river road. they left the car at green meadow park in the gravel lot. come on russel shouted this path leads right down to the River. Last one in yelled clint is a rotten egg! wait called Jin we forgot the Red Wrigglers.

© SRA/McGraw-Hill. Permission is granted to reproduce this page for classroom use.

Appendix

Lesson/Title	ISBN	Publisher
Lesson 1 *The Golden Bracelet*	0823413624	Holiday House
Lesson 2 *The Dragon Kite*	0152241973	Harcourt Brace
Lesson 3 *Androcles and the Lion*	0152033556	Harcourt Brace
Lesson 4 *Pedro and the Monkey*	0688137431	William Morrow
Lesson 5 *The Faithful Friend*	0689824580	Simon & Schuster
Lesson 6 *In the Beginning: Creation Stories from Around the World*	0152387404	Harcourt Brace
Lesson 7 *The Great Race*	0761303057	Millbrook Press
Lesson 8 *A Ring of Tricksters*	0590473743	Scholastic
Lesson 9 *Medusa*	0060279044	HarperCollins
Lesson 10 *The Sea King's Daughter*	0689807597	Simon & Schuster
Lesson 11 *Favorite Norse Myths*	0590480472	Scholastic
Lesson 12 *Kids at Work*	0395797268	Clarion Books
Lesson 13 *The Great Kapok Tree: A Tale of the Amazon Rain Forest*	0152026142	Harcourt Brace
Lesson 14 *The Most Beautiful Roof in the World*	0152008977	Gulliver Books

Lesson/Title	ISBN	Publisher
■ Lesson 15 *The Missing 'Gator of Gumbo Limbo*	0785707883	Econo-Clad
■ Lesson 16 *The Jazz Man*	0689717679	Aladin Paperbacks
■ Lesson 17 *The Most Beautiful Place in the World*	0394804244	Random House
■ Lesson 18 *Run Away Home*	0590467522	Scholastic
■ Lesson 19 *Number the Stars*	0440227534	Laureleaf
■ Lesson 20 *Red Scarf Girl*	0064462080	HarperCollins